# Ask for the Angel

## Working With Angels

Ira Milligan

Copyright © 2023 by Ira Milligan

ISBN: 979-8-9877359-4-7 (paperback)

All rights reserved. This book is protected under the copyright laws of the United States of America. No part of this book may be reproduced in any form, except for the inclusion of brief quotations in a review or article, without written permission from the author or publisher.

> Published by: Servant Ministries, Inc.
> PO Box 1120
> Tioga, LA 71477

All references to Greek word definitions are from Strong's Exhaustive Concordance, Thomas Nelson Publishers, 1990. Unless otherwise indicated, all Scripture references are taken from the New King James Version. Copyright 1979, 1980, 1982 by Thomas Nelson, Inc. Used by permission. All rights reserved. *Italics* are used throughout for clarity of expression and for emphasis. They are used in select portions of scriptural quotations for the same reason

This book is dedicated to Anita Smart, who asked me to write a book on angels, and when it was not forthcoming, gently reminded me that I promised her that I would!

I wish to express my heartfelt thanks to Robert Goins for his help. His expertise in computers has been invaluable!

The cover design is by James Nesbit (www. Jnesbit.com).

As always, I am eternally grateful for those loyal, faithful, friends whose prayers and financial support has enabled me to give myself continually to prayer, ministry, and the publication of the many revelations that God has given me over the 60 plus years that I have served Him.

# Contents

| | | |
|---|---|---|
| 1 | Ask for the Angel | 3 |
| 2 | The Ministry of Angels | 13 |
| 3 | Working with Angels | 21 |
| 4 | The Number and Nature of Angels | 37 |
| 5 | Discerning Angels | 49 |
| 6 | The Angel of His Presence | 57 |
| 7 | Messenger Angels | 67 |
| 8 | Asking Specifically | 79 |
| 9 | Evil Angels | 121 |
| 10 | Angel Worship Forbidden | 133 |
| 11 | Tidbits | 143 |

# Ask for the Angel

# Chapter One

## Ask for the Angel

As we travel across the country to minister my wife Judy usually drives while I sleep, pray, or simply observe the countryside as it passes by. We were ministering in a church in western Missouri and while there we received an invitation to minister in a church we had never ministered in before, located in a city a little north of where we were. The next day, as she drove us there, I asked the Lord, *"What do you want me to tell these people where we are going?"* He immediately answered, *"Tell them it doesn't hurt to ask for the angel"*. Then He reminded me of the scripture where Jesus told Peter to put up his sword after Peter tried to defend Him from the priests and Roman solders who came to arrest Him:

> But Jesus said to him, "Put up your sword in its place, for all who take the sword will perish by the sword. *Or do you think that I cannot now pray to My Father, and He will provide Me with more than twelve legions of angel?* How then could the scriptures be fulfilled, that it must happen thus?" (Matthew 26:52-54; italics mine)

The Holy Spirit then reminded me of what the devil quoted to Jesus when He was being tempted in the wilderness,

> Then the devil took Him up into the holy city, set Him on the pinnacle of the temple, and said to Him, "If You are the Son of God, throw Yourself down. *For it is written: 'He shall give His angels charge over you,' and, 'In their hands they shall bear you up, Lest you dash your foot against a stone'.*" Jesus said to him, "It is written again, 'You shall not tempt the Lord your God'." (Matthew 4:5-7; italics mine)

As God brought these scriptures to my mind, I realized something that I had never thought of before—if Jesus, the Son of God, had to ask for the angels to protect Him, even though Psalms 91 gave them a specific charge to keep Him in *all* His ways—how much more do *we* have to ask for their help? It is a mistake to take God's promises for granted! We should ask for their fulfillment just like our Master said that He could do, although He declined the privilege for our sake.

This Psalm's promise is unmistakable! "No evil shall befall you"—but they arrested Him with impunity!

> No evil shall befall you, Nor shall any plague come near your dwelling; For He shall give His angels charge over you, To keep you in all your ways. In their hands they shall bear you up, Lest you dash your foot against a stone. (Psalm 91:10-12)

The angels were given a charge to take good care of Him but their hands were tied because He declined to ask for their help. Jesus said His

Father would send Him twelve legions of angels if He asked for them! A Roman legion was between 4,000 to 6,000 soldiers, including a calvary of horsemen in each legion. That would be as many as 72,000 warrior angels! That many could have easily intervened and defeated His antagonists but then He would not have completed His mission to offer Himself as an acceptable sacrifice for our sins.

How much needless trouble have we suffered simply because we failed to ask our Heavenly Father to provide the angels that we needed? How much lack have we endured even though God has an abundant supply of everything we could possibly want or need? God has promised to meet our every need—whether it is material things, such as money or food—or intangible things, such as directions or answers to perplexing problems, yet, all too often His promises go unfulfilled. Why? Because we fail to ask for the angels that He created to fulfill His word and accomplish His works! James admonished us about this. He said, "You do not have because you do not ask" (James 4:2).

Every promise that God makes or has made is conditional. Although the conditions may vary from one promise to the next, one condition that applies to almost every one of them is this—we must ask for their fulfillment. We should not, *and cannot*, take God's promises for granted. Why? Because we must justify God in giving us what He has promised by meeting His conditions. Otherwise, if He gave us what we want or need without being justified by our obedience, He would then be obligated to do the same thing for everyone else in the world.

Malachi asked, "Have we not all one Father? Has not one God created us?" (Malachi 2:19). Because God is impartial in fulfilling His promises, if He foolishly provided for us without requiring us to meet His conditions, then He would have to do the same thing that He did for us for everyone else in the world—and God is not foolish—so, that is not going to happen. One way or another, we either meet His conditions, whether they are stated or implied, or we will do without!

One can see this process of asking first, then

receiving God's answer in return, in Jacob's first vision of angels,

> Now Jacob went out from Beersheba and went toward Haran. So, he came to a certain place and stayed there all night, because the sun had set. And he took one of the stones of that place and put it at his head, and he lay down in that place to sleep. Then he dreamed, and behold, a ladder was set up on the earth, and its top reached to heaven; and there the angels of God were ascending and descending on it. (Genesis 28:10-12)

Notice that the angels were first ascending, then descending! Why ascend first? Because angels are always present here on earth, patiently waiting to receive our petitions, prayers and sacrifices to take them to the Father. Afterward, they return with His answers and provisions. John describes this process in the book of Revelation:

> Then another angel, having a golden censer, came and stood at the altar. He was given much incense, that he should offer it with the prayers of all the saints

upon the golden altar which was before the throne. *And the smoke of the incense, with the prayers of the saints, ascended before God from the angel's hand.* (Revelation 8:3-4; italics mine)

God's precious saints have cried out for justice for hundreds of years—seemingly without being heard. Why? Because the world cannot be held accountable for its trespasses without sufficient witnesses (see Deuteronomy 17:6). Once the gospel of the Kingdom has been proclaimed throughout all the world with accompanying signs and wonders, their accumulated prayers will be answered. There is no shelf-life on prayer nor is there a statute of limitations on sin. The saints' prayers are not being ignored. Once the world's iniquity is full and it has had two or more witnesses, justice *will* be served! Jesus said,

> If I had not come and spoken to them, they would have no sin, but now they have no excuse for their sin. He who hates Me hates My Father also. If I had not done among them the works which

no one else did, they would have no sin; but now they have seen and also hated both Me and My Father. (John 15:22-24)

Jesus confirmed this order (of angels first ascending and then descending) when He prophesied to Nathanael that as he followed Him, he would see the heavens opened and angels ascending and descending as they ministered to Him,

Nathanael answered and said to Him, "Rabbi, You are the Son of God! You are the King of Israel!" Jesus answered and said to him, "Because I said to you, 'I saw you under the fig tree,' do you believe? You will see greater things than these." And He said to him, "Most assuredly, *I say to you, hereafter you shall see heaven open, and the angels of God ascending and descending upon the Son of Man"*. (John 1:49-51; italics mine)

As we continue our study, we will see that angels are active (or should be, if we ask for them) in nearly every aspect of our lives. There are specific angels gifted and commissioned to do specific tasks but *all* of them are available for

## Ask for the Angel

the asking because the Bible says they are all ministering spirits sent forth to minister for those who will inherit salvation (see Hebrews 1:14). If you are a child of God, the angels are ready and willing to assist you in any and every way that you need them to. Just ask!

# Ask for the Angel

# Chapter Two

## The Ministry of Angels

One night after going to bed, just before falling asleep, the Lord suddenly asked me this question: *"What was the name of the angel, or angels, that went before Joshua when he went into the Promised Land?"* Although I was completely surprised by the question, I knew that He was referring to the angel whom Joshua met at Jericho before they began their seven-day march around the city:

> And it came to pass, when Joshua was by Jericho, that he lifted his eyes and looked, and behold, a Man stood opposite him with His sword drawn in His hand. And Joshua went to Him and said to Him, "Are You for us or for our adversaries?" So, He said, "No, but as

Commander of the army of the Lord I have now come." And Joshua fell on his face to the earth and worshiped, and said to Him, "What does my Lord say to His servant?" Then the Commander of the Lord's army said to Joshua, "Take your sandal off your foot, for the place where you stand is holy." And Joshua did so. (Joshua 5:13-15)

I was puzzled by the question and my answer was, *"Lord, I don't know. The Bible doesn't say."* To which He replied, *"Toronto"*. Then I was *really* surprised! *"Toronto!"* I thought, *"Tomorrow I'll have to look that name up and see what it means"*. Then I realized that Toronto was an Indian name and I didn't have any way to look it up, but as I thought about it God continued the conversation and said, *"The angel of dread"*.

Later, I discovered the literal meaning of the name Toronto is *"The meeting place"*. So, the angel that revealed himself to Joshua, as he began leading Israel into Canaan, put the dread of meeting Joshua and the armies of Israel upon the Canaanites, just as God had promised that He would do:

> No man shall be able to stand against you; the Lord your God will put the dread of you and the fear of you upon all the land where you tread, just as He has said to you. (Deuteronomy 11:25)

When Joshua's two spies went into the land and met the harlot that hid them from their pursuers, she explained the reason she was willing to hide them,

> Now before they [*the two spies*] lay down, she came up to them on the roof and said to the men: "I know that the Lord has given you the land, that the terror of you has fallen on us, and that all the inhabitants of the land are fainthearted because of you. For we have heard how the Lord dried up the water of the Red Sea for you when you came out of Egypt... And as soon as we heard these things, our hearts melted; neither did there remain any more courage in anyone because of you, for the Lord your God, He is God in heaven above and on earth beneath". (Joshua 2:8-11)

Besides the obvious lessons to be gleaned from these passages, there is one that is easily overlooked, Joshua didn't presume to command the angel, rather he bowed before him and asked him what he should do, and in the process called himself the angel's servant! I mention this because some ministers are teaching that we are supposed to assume authority over angels and command them to do our bidding. This is a dangerous heresy! Who, in his right mind, would presume to command an angel who has the ability to paralyze an entire nation by filling their hearts with fear and dread? The Bible says we are made "a little lower than the angels", and the writer of Hebrews said, "Now beyond all contradiction the lesser is blessed by the better". (Hebrews 7:7)

> But one testified in a certain place, saying: "What is man that You are mindful of him, Or the son of man that You take care of him? You have made him a little lower than the angels; You have crowned him with glory and honor, And set him over the works of

Your hands". (Hebrews 2:5-7)

The writer went on to say that even Jesus was made lower than the angels (see Hebrews 2:9). That explains why Jesus said that He could ask His Father (not command the angels) and He would provide more than enough angels to protect Him.

When Gabriel was sent to Zacharias to announce his wife's conception of John the Baptist, Zacharias foolishly questioned his word.

> And Zacharias said to the angel, "How shall I know this? For I am an old man, and my wife is well advanced in years." And the angel answered and said to him, "I am Gabriel, who stands in the presence of God, and was sent to speak to you and bring you these glad tidings. But behold, you will be mute and not able to speak until the day these things take place, because you did not believe my words which will be fulfilled in their own time." (Luke 1:18-20)

To paraphrase Gabriel's reply, he said, "You question my word? You won't question anyone else's because you will be dumb until they come to pass!" As we can see, it would not be very wise to try to order that guy around! He might take offense at your arrogance. Angels are "greater in power and might" than we are! Even the angels themselves recognize the proper spiritual chain of command and rigidly adhere to it.

> Whereas angels, who are greater in power and might [*than men*], do not bring a reviling accusation against them [*principalities and powers of the spiritual realm*] before the Lord. (2 Peter 2:11)

When Joshua saw the angel at Jericho, he asked him whose side he was on, to which the angel replied *"No"*. He wasn't taking sides or receiving orders from either side. He got his orders straight from the Throne Room—from the Father, Himself!

As we continue, we will see that it is important for us to discern what the angels' commission is and work with them to fulfill it, rather than think they are there to meet our expectations. This Commander had been given orders to put the fear and dread of meeting up with Joshua upon the inhabitants of Canaan. As long as Israel stayed in God's good graces, they could depend upon him doing exactly as he was instructed to do. But when they slipped up at Jericho and allowed sin into the camp, and afterward went out to war against Ai, the angel put up his sword and watched them flee before their enemies! The irony of this story is *Ai* means *"ruin"!*

Every promise of God is conditional, and one condition that applies to every promise He makes or has made is that we avoid covetousness, which is idolatry. (see Colossians 3:5)

> And they returned to Joshua and said to him, "Do not let all the people go up, but let about two or three thousand men go up and attack Ai. Do not weary all the people there, for the people of Ai are few." So about three thousand men went up there from the people, but they fled before the men of Ai. (Joshua 7:3-4)

Although we cannot legitimately command angels of our own accord, when we pray in other tongues the Holy Spirit can (and often does) commission them to minister either with or for us, according to the need. Since we don't always know what the future holds, and what kind of assistance we may need, the Holy Spirit intercedes for us as we pray in the Spirit. We can be sure this is one of the reasons that Paul told the Corinthians, "I thank my God I speak with tongues more than you all". (1 Corinthians 14:18; see also Romans 8:26). Paul's exciting, powerful ministry required a *lot* of angelic assistance, and in some really unexpected ways!

# Chapter Three

## Working with Angels

The Lord has established His throne in heaven, And His kingdom rules over all. *Bless the Lord, you His angels, Who excel in strength, who do His word, Heeding the voice of His word.* (Psalm 103:19-20; italics mine)

It has been said that the Kingdom of God is "voice-activated". Obviously, this is an over-simplification, but it is at least partially true. Actually, there are several things besides the spoken word that activate God's Kingdom, including fasting, prayer and sacrifice. But, *if there is* one single word that describes what activates and releases God's power into the earthly realm, it is *obedience*, rather than voice. Nevertheless, as the scripture above says, *when we speak God's word in obedience to the Holy Sprit's inspiration,* angels are activated!

In the scripture above, the word "voice" is translated from the Hebrew *"kole"* and means to *"call aloud"*, or *"sound"*. This principle, of the angels responding to God's spoken word and performing it, is seen in the story of Jesus cursing the fig tree:

> And seeing from afar a fig tree having leaves, He went to see if perhaps He would find something on it. When He came to it, He found nothing but leaves, for it was not the season for figs. In response *Jesus said to it, "Let no one eat fruit from you ever again." And His disciples heard it.* (Mark 11:13-14; italics mine)

Jesus spoke aloud, and "His disciples heard it", but they were not the only ones who heard what He said. Jesus only spoke and did what He saw His Father say and do, so, His word was God's word. Since angels heed "the voice of His word", when He cursed the fig tree an angel immediately smote it at its roots.

> Now in the morning, as they passed by, they saw the fig tree dried up from the

roots. And Peter, remembering, said to Him, "Rabbi, look! The fig tree which You cursed has withered away." So. Jesus answered and said to them, "Have faith in God. For assuredly, I say to you, whoever says to this mountain, 'Be removed and be cast into the sea,' and does not doubt in his heart, but believes that those things he says will be done, he will have whatever he says". (Mark 11:20-23)

We are using this passage to illustrate a kingdom principle of one of the ways that we can work with angels, but in passing we should note that it is vitally important to be careful to watch what we say. We often say things in the heat of passion, and in that moment we sincerely believe and mean what we say, therefore our words impact those we speak to in fearsome ways. Once we have time to think about what we said, we may regret saying it, but the damage is already done: "Death and life are in the power of the tongue". (Proverbs 18:21). The angel didn't wait for a second confirmation before he acted on Christ's word and smote the fig tree!

If we are properly attuned to the Father's will through the Holy Spirit's guidance, many times we can discern an angel's presence and the purpose for him being there. Such is the case in the story of Jesus' visit to the pool of Bethesda:

> For an angel went down at a certain time into the pool and stirred up the water; then whoever stepped in first, after the stirring of the water, was made well of whatever disease he had. Now a certain man was there who had an infirmity thirty-eight years. When Jesus saw him lying there, and knew that he already had been in that condition a long time, He said to him, "Do you want to be made well?" The sick man answered Him, "Sir, I have no man to put me into the pool when the water is stirred up; but while I am coming, another steps down before me." Jesus said to him, "Rise, take up your bed and walk." And immediately the man was made well, took up his bed, and walked.... (John 5:4-9)

There are several things in this scriptural

passage that we need to analyze. First, the setting is this: a specific, healing angel is sent by the Father to heal only one person, at a specific time (which was predetermined by the Father). When the angel arrives on the scene, since he is invisible, he has to stir up the water so the people will know that he is present. Then he heals the first person who responds and gets into the water. His mission completed, he leaves and goes on his way (probably to his next assignment). In this story, although the angel has arrived at the poolside, he has not yet disturbed the water to alert those who are waiting that he is there. Jesus, who is sensitive to the Holy Spirit's guidance, discerns both his presence and purpose.

Looking around, Jesus saw a man who had been there for thirty-eight, long difficult years. This time is important because it speaks of repentance! Thirty-eight years is how long the children of Israel wasted away in the wilderness until all the old men were dead. This story is a living (hidden) parable. The number of years illustrates the man's repentant condition. He has put off the "old man" by sincerely repenting of the decadent lifestyle that he lived before becoming sick!

> And the time we took to come from Kadesh Barnea until we crossed over the Valley of the Zered was *thirty-eight years*, until all the generation of the [*unbelieving, disobedient*] men of war was consumed from the midst of the camp, just as the Lord had sworn to them. (Deuteronomy 2:14; italics mine)

When Jesus said to him, "Rise, take up your bed and walk.", the angel immediately responded to His word and healed the man. Then John tells us that after this happened, "...Jesus found [*the healed man*] in the temple, and said to him, 'See, you have been made well. Sin no more, lest a worse thing come upon you'." (John 5:14)

Sin opened the door for his sickness. Repentance qualified him for healing. To fall back into the same pattern of sin would open the door for the demons of infirmity to return and make him sick again, and Jesus assured him that his last sickness would be worse than the first. (see Acts 10:28; Luke 11:24-26)

Apparently, when the disciples saw that He

only healed one person instead of healing them all, as He did on so many other occasions, they wondered why, so, Jesus explained the reason He acted the way that He did.

> Then Jesus answered and said to them, "Most assuredly, I say to you, the Son can do nothing of Himself, but what He sees the Father do; for whatever He does, the Son also does in like manner. For the Father loves the Son, and shows Him all things that He Himself does; and He will show Him greater works than these, that you may marvel". (John 5:19-20)

Regardless of the reason for His explanation, we need to realize that like Joshua before Him, He worked within the angel's commission instead of expecting the angel to work within His. Peter said, "Known unto God are all his works from the beginning of the world" (Acts 15:18; KJV). We can do nothing of ourselves. Since angels fulfill the Father's word and do His work, the more we can discern His will and timing and work with them, the more successful we will be in getting the people saved, healed and delivered.

Another important point that Jesus gives us in this story is that here, and in several other Scriptures, He said that it wasn't Himself, but rather it was His Father who was the One doing the works. We often hear someone attributing a specific miracle of healing to the Holy Spirit, but Jesus said it is His Father doing it. How? By His angels. All things are created by His word, and as we discussed previously, David said the angels "do His word, Heeding the voice of His word". This scripture is so important that it bears repeating!

> The Lord has established His throne in heaven, And His kingdom rules over all. Bless the Lord, you *His angels,* Who excel in strength, *who do His word, Heeding the voice of His word.* (Psalm 103:19-20; italics mine)

John said, "For there are three that bear witness in heaven: the Father, the Word, and the Holy Spirit; and these three are one" (1 John 5:7). Perhaps the following is an over-simplification, but John taught us that the Son (Word) *declares,* the Holy Spirit *shows* or *reveals,* and the Father *does the works* (through the mediation of angels—see John 1:18; 16:13; 14:10; also, Galatians 3:19). This is what Jesus is referring to when He said, "

> My Father has been working until now, and I have been working... Most assuredly, I say to you, the Son can do nothing of Himself, but what He sees the Father do; for whatever He does, the Son also does in like manner. For the Father loves the Son, and shows Him [*by the Holy Spirit*] all things that He Himself does... [*through the ministry of angels*]. (John 5:17, 19-20)

As Jesus was (in the days of His flesh), so are we. We can do nothing of ourselves, but the Father shows us, by the Holy Spirit, what His angels are commissioned and sent to do so that we can work with them to manifest His works here on the earth.

There are many things that angels cannot do without our participation. On the other hand, we can accomplish very little without their help! Being successful in ministry, regardless of what type of ministry we are called to do, requires teamwork. Jesus always sent the disciples out "two by two" and the apostles always worked in teams, such as Paul and Barnabas (see Mark 6:7; Luke 10:1; also see Acts 15:32; 2 Corinthians 13:1). We must learn to work with both our fellow ministers and the Father's angels if we want to be consistently successful as we minister.

We can learn from Samson's failure. Since angels do the Father's bidding, it is more than probable that it was a powerful angel that made him incredibly strong and enabled him to perform the supernatural feats of strength that he did. Although Samson obviously worked with angels, he could have blown a trumpet and rallied an army of Israelites to fight with him, as those who came before him did, but he trusted solely in his gift, to his downfall. Samson's life is a recipe for disaster. He foolishly worked alone, with neither backup nor accountability.

We can also learn from Elijah and Elisha. Elijah was another loner, and although he was somewhat successful in overcoming Jezebel's corruption of Israel, Elisha was able to accomplish far more than Elijah did. Although there is more than one reason for Elisha's success, it was partially because he was willing to work with others. Samuel was another highly successful prophet who was a team worker. He was instrumental in raising up a whole company of prophets, and in many ways, he was David's spiritual mentor (see 1 Samuel 19:18-20). Regardless of how great our individual potential is, it is exponentially greater when we work as a team.

When we assemble together, the Bible says there are "an innumerable company of angels" present. This means there is no shortage of laborers available to do the work. The more we can discern their presence and purpose, and work with them, the more successful we will be in our endeavors to accomplish the Father's will and work.

> Are they not all ministering spirits sent forth to minister for [Gk: *dia*: – *channel or through*] those who will inherit salvation? (Hebrews 1:14)

As the scripture above shows, angels work both *through* and *alongside* (or with) God's ministers. Most anointings appear to be angels working *through* them, whereas the angels who perform their spoken word are working *with* them. For example, angels of supplication (or intercession) enable prayer warriors to pray with far greater potency than just praying by the Holy Spirit anointing, alone. An angel of intercession is seen working through Jesus when He was praying in the garden immediately prior to His arrest:

> And He was withdrawn from them about a stone's throw, and He knelt down and prayed, saying, "Father, if it is Your will, take this cup away from Me; nevertheless, not My will, but Yours, be done." *Then an angel appeared to Him from heaven, strengthening Him. And being in agony, He prayed more earnestly...* (Luke 22:41-44; italics mine)

On the other hand, the story of Jesus healing the Roman centurion's servant gives us a perfect example of angels working with Him, performing His spoken word:

> Now when Jesus had entered Capernaum, a centurion came to Him, pleading with Him, saying, "Lord, my servant is lying at home paralyzed,

dreadfully tormented." And Jesus said to him, "I will come and heal him." The centurion answered and said, "Lord, I am not worthy that You should come under my roof. But only speak a word, and my servant will be healed. *For I also am a man under authority, having soldiers under me.* And I say to this one, 'Go,' and he goes; and to another, 'Come,' and he comes; and to my servant, 'Do this,' and he does it." When Jesus heard it, He marveled, and said to those who followed, "Assuredly, I say to you, I have not found such great faith, not even in Israel!" …. *Then Jesus said to the centurion, "Go your way; and as you have believed, so let it be done for you."* And his servant was healed that same hour. (Matthew 8:5-10, 13; italics mine)

The Roman centurion understood that Jesus was a person under the authority of a higher power, like himself. He recognized that Jesus' power came from above, and like himself, He only needed to give the command and the job would be done. We are also under authority, and, through our submission to Jesus' Lordship, we have the same privilege of hearing and speaking the Father's word that Christ demonstrated.

Jesus said, "Most assuredly, I say to you, he who believes in Me, the works that I do he will do also; and greater works than these he will do, because I go to My Father" (John 14:12). If we want to do the same works that Jesus did, we must use the same tactics that He used, and He only said and did what He saw His Father saying and doing.

Just knowing the written word and quoting it is not hearing the Father and speaking His word, as some teach! God's word is alive. Among other things, the written word declares God's covenant promises and reveals His ways and His will—which enable us to judge what we hear to determine whether it is indeed God's voice or not, but it is a mistake to think that just because we can quote a written promise that God is going to automatically fulfill it.

Every promise has conditions that must be fulfilled and just knowing and quoting a promise does not satisfy them. Jesus said, "Man shall not live by bread alone, but by every word that *proceeds* from the mouth of God". (Matthew 4:4; italics mine)

Notice that He said, "that proceeds" (present-tense), not "that has proceeded" (past-tense)! Jesus is quoting from Deuteronomy 8:3, and the Hebrew and Greek words that are translated *proceeds* in both Testaments refer to an active, present-tense action. Jesus is alive and His word is alive.

God requires us to have a devoted, loving, living, active relationship which Him—not just an intellectual relationship with Him through His written word. In fact, that kind of relationship can be very deceiving. It can even be detrimental to our eternal well-being when we stand before the judgment seat of Christ at the last day.

> Not everyone who says to Me, 'Lord, Lord,' shall enter the kingdom of heaven, but he who does the will of My Father in heaven. Many will say to Me in that day, 'Lord, Lord, have we not prophesied in Your name, cast out demons in Your name, and done many wonders in Your name?' And then I will declare to them, 'I

never knew you; depart from Me, you who practice lawlessness!' (Matthew 7:21-23)

Angels are ever-present, ready and willing to aid us as we minister. Their only limitations are those we place upon them through our lack of understanding or our unbelief. Learning to discern their presence and purpose will greatly increase our effectiveness in ministry.

Then He [Jesus] said to them, "The harvest truly is great, but the laborers are few; therefore, pray the Lord of the harvest to send out laborers [*both men and angels*] into His harvest." (Luke 10:2)

# Chapter Four

# The Number and Nature of Angels

But you have come to Mount Zion and to the city of the living God, the heavenly Jerusalem, *to an innumerable company of angels.* (Hebrews 12:22; italics mine)

Angels are active in every aspect of our lives. Every one of us has a personal angel assigned from birth who always sees and comprehends our Heavenly Father's will for our lives. This angel (who is traditionally known as our *guardian angel*), is instrumental in helping us reach our full potential in life. Obviously, he has the power to cause harm to anyone who mistreats the child he watches over because Jesus warned us about his presence,

> Take heed that you do not despise one of these little ones, for I say to you that in heaven their angels always see the face of My Father who is in heaven. (Matthew 18:10)

Our face reveals our heart. If we have a happy face, we have a happy heart; sad face, sad heart; scolding face, angry heart; etc. So, when Jesus says that our personal angel always beholds our Heavenly Father's face, He is saying the angel is in constant contact with God and knows His heart's desire for our lives. In addition to our guardian angel, as we walk with the Lord and mature in Christ, we are assigned others who work with and through us to accomplish the Father's good and perfect will.

Later, we will see there are specialist angels who excel in certain, specific ministries. So, our individual calling determines which angels are assigned to work with us. As we saw in the second chapter, Toronto was assigned to go before Joshua to smite the Canaanites with fear and dread to make them fall before Israel's army as they invaded the land.

Angels are not limited to assisting us in the ministry. Besides ministering *with* and *through* us, they also minister *to* and *for* us! They often minister directly to our needs. The Scripture says that angels ministered to Jesus immediately after He defeated Satan and ended His forty-day fast in the wilderness.

> Then the devil left Him, and behold, angels came and ministered to Him. (Matthew 4:11)

Fasting makes one physically weak, so, among other things, they strengthened Him and possibly even brought Him food, as they did for Elijah when he was exhausted after fleeing from Jezebel. At that time an angel brought him "a cake baked on coals, and a jar of water"—not once but twice!

> Then as [*Elijah*] lay and slept under a broom tree, suddenly an angel touched

him, and said to him, "Arise and eat." Then he looked, and there by his head was a cake baked on coals, and a jar of water. So he ate and drank, and lay down again. And the angel of the Lord came back the second time, and touched him, and said, "Arise and eat, because the journey is too great for you." So, he arose, and ate and drank; and he went in the strength of that food forty days and forty nights as far as Horeb, the mountain of God. (1 Kings 19:5-8)

Angels are not far, far away, way up in the heavens, waiting to be sent down when we cry to God for help. They dwell right here among us. They move like lightning, being instant in response when summoned to our aid (see Ezekiel 1:14). They are always present and active in our lives, as David testified after they helped him escape from Abimelech in the Philistine territory.

This poor man cried out, and the Lord heard him, And saved him out of all his troubles. *The angel of the Lord encamps all around those who fear Him,* and delivers them. (Psalm 34:6-7; italics mine)

Another insight into the nature of angels that the Bible gives us is that they do not marry, as humans do. In describing the resurrection of the just, Jesus said,

Neither can they [*the saints who are in the first resurrection*] die any more: for *they are equal unto the angels*; and are the children of God, being the children of the resurrection.... *For when they rise from the dead, they neither marry nor are given in marriage, but are like angels in heaven.* (Luke 20:36; Mark 12:25; italics mine)

Being equal to the angels is not the same as being equal to God, but like them, in the resurrection we will share many of our Heavenly Father's wonderful attributes. We serve an awesome God! He is *invisible, eternal, immortal, immutable, omniscient, omnipotent* and *omnipresent*. Besides manifesting the Father's heart, angels also share several of His seven, divine attributes. For instance, all angels are invisible unless there is a need for them to manifest themselves as humans. Also, they are both eternal and immortal.

Angels also have supernatural knowledge and understanding, although they aren't omniscient the way God is. They obviously learn through experience the same as we do because Peter said that the "angels desire to look into" the hidden mysteries that the prophets of old prophesied that are now revealed as part of the gospel covenant,

> To them [*the former prophets*] it was revealed that, not to themselves, but to us they were ministering the things which now have been reported to you through those who have preached the gospel to you by the Holy Spirit sent from heaven—things which angels desire to look into. (1 Peter 1:12)

Angels also have supernatural strength (although they are not omnipotent). Peter said they were "greater in power and might" than we are (see 2 Peter 2:11). In fact, they are *much* greater! One angel killed 185,000 enemy warriors in a single night, even singling out and killing the officers and chief men in the process! (See 2 Chronicles 32:21)

> Then the angel of the Lord went out, and killed in the camp of the Assyrians one hundred and eighty-five thousand; and when people arose early in the morning, there were the corpses—all dead. (Isaiah 37:36)

In Scripture, some angels have wings, but most of them have the appearance of ordinary men, in fact, so ordinary that we may meet them and not even know they are angels. The writer of Hebrews cautioned us about this, "Do not forget to entertain strangers, for by so doing some have unwittingly entertained angels" (Hebrews 13:2).

When God sent two angels to Sodom to test the people to confirm that the evil reports that He had received were true, the perverted men of Sodom obviously didn't know that the men were angels. Also, even though Lot was sheltering them, it is doubtful that he knew they were, either—that is, until he witnessed them blind the wicked men who were trying to force him to compromise and participate with them in their perversion—then he knew (see Genesis 19:1-11).

The angels who have wings appear to be angels of high rank, such as seraphim (or seraphs) and cherubim (or cherubs). When Moses built the Ark of the Covenant, he made two cherubs whose wings covered the mercy seat:

> The cherubim spread out their wings above and covered the mercy seat with their wings. They faced one another; the faces of the cherubim were toward the mercy seat. (Exodus 37:9)

The cherubim that appeared to Ezekiel had four faces and two pairs of wings. They also had hands under their wings:

> Also, from within it came the likeness of four living creatures. And this was their appearance: they had the likeness of a man. Each one had four faces, and each one had four wings. Their legs were straight, and the soles of their feet were

like the soles of calves' feet. They sparkled like the color of burnished bronze. The hands of a man were under their wings on their four sides; and each of the four had faces and wings.... As for the likeness of their faces, each had *the face of a man*; each of the four had *the face of a lion* on the right side, each of the four had *the face of an ox* on the left side, and each of the four had *the face of an eagle.* (Ezekiel 1:5-8, 10; italics mine)

The four faces depict the four ministry anointings. In the order that Ezekiel gives them to us—the man represents the pastor-teacher anointing, the lion symbolizes the apostolic, the ox the evangelistic and the eagle depicts the prophetic. In Revelation, John described four living creatures that resemble cherubim, the exception being that each face belonged to an individual creature, and each one had six wings (see Revelation 4:6-8). Whether these creatures were angels or not, John doesn't say.

The only occurrence of seraphim in Scripture are the angels that Isaiah saw in the temple above God's throne. They also had six wings. One of them took a coal of fire and touched Isaiah's lips with it to purify his speech, which is appropriate because seraph means "the fiery ones" (see Isaiah 6:1-6).

Another aspect of angels is the fact that those who sinned in the beginning cannot repent and change their ways, the way we can. They are delivered "into chains of darkness"—which does not mean that they are imprisoned and cannot work and do evil in this world—it means they cannot repent and become children of light, as humans can. They are sentenced to dwell in the realms of darkness, forever. (see 2 Peter 2:4; Matthew 8:29; 1 Thessalonians 5:5)

So, God's mighty angelic armies are composed of a host of supernatural, invincible warriors. His workforce is readily available and fully equipped, and capable of aiding us in carrying out His commands. His supply is without measure or limit, so, there is *nothing* that can keep us from doing His will and carrying out His orders if we sincerely believe His word. The angel Gabriel told Mary, "For with God nothing will be impossible", and Jesus said, "According to your faith let it be to you." Therefore, by faith in God Paul was able to say, "I can do all things through Christ who strengthens me". We need only believe and obey to accomplish all that the Master commissions us to do. (see Luke 1:37; Matthew 9:29; Philippians 4:13)

> Now may the God of peace who brought up our Lord Jesus from the dead, that great Shepherd of the sheep, through the blood of the everlasting covenant, make you complete in every good work to do His will, working in you what is well pleasing in His sight, through Jesus Christ, to whom be glory forever and ever. Amen. (Hebrews 13:20-21)

# Ask for the Angel

# Chapter Five

# Discerning Angels

2 Kings, Chapter 6, gives us an interesting story of one of Syria's attempts to engage Israel in war during the time when Elisha the prophet was Israel's watchman. Elisha repeatedly foiled their attempts by informing the king of Israel of Syria's immediate battle plans. The Syrian king thought he had a spy in his camp but one of his servants informed him that his problem wasn't an internal spy, but rather Elisha was the one who was revealing his secrets to the king of Israel. So, the Syrian king sent an army to arrest Elisha, but he obviously didn't consider the fact that if Elisha knew of his plans to invade Israel, he would certainly know about his plans to capture him!

The results of the Syrian king's futile efforts are rather amusing!

> And when the servant of the man of God arose early and went out, there was an army, surrounding the city with horses and chariots. And his servant said to him, "Alas, my master! What shall we do?" So he answered, "Do not fear, for those who are with us are more than those who are with them." And Elisha prayed, and said, "Lord, I pray, open his eyes that he may see." Then the Lord opened the eyes of the young man, and he saw. And behold, the mountain was full of horses and chariots of fire all around Elisha. So, when the Syrians came down to him, Elisha prayed to the Lord, and said, "Strike this people, I pray, with blindness." And He struck them with blindness according to the word of Elisha. (2 Kings 6:15-18)

In response to Elisha's prayer, God opened the servant's eyes and enabled him to see into the supernatural realm, and then when Elisha prayed the second time, God blinded the eyes of the entire Syrian army! As we saw in the last chapter, faith and obedience are the keys to success. Elisha, like his master Elijah before him, was a man who was subject to the same temptations that we are, yet his prayers were so powerful and his prophetic warnings were so accurate and timely that he subdued whole armies and saved the nation of Israel from the armies of Syria more than once—all because he believed in God and knew how to ask for and work with the angels! (See James 5:17)

This biblical story illustrates the two primary things that we have discussed thus far; believing in the abundant presence and supernatural ability of angels and the necessity of asking God for their assistance. But we need to go beyond just knowing they are available. We need to be able to discern their presence and know their purpose!

Although some angels can manifest themselves physically as humans, in their natural state all of them are invisible. Because of this, the Holy Spirit uses three specific ways to reveal their presence to us. One is by allowing us to *see* them, as He did for Elisha's servant in the passage above. There is nothing hidden in the spirit world that is invisible to God. The Bible says, "And there is no creature hidden from His sight, but all things are naked and open to the eyes of Him to whom we must give account". (Hebrews 4:13)

The Holy Spirit may also reveal angels to us by giving us "a word of knowledge". A word of knowledge is one of the nine manifestations of the Holy Spirit. He either speaks to us and tells us they are there, or, in a way that cannot be explained, He just causes us to *know* they are there, and often know the reason why they are present (see 1 Corinthians 12:8).

Another way the Holy Spirit reveals that angels are present is by allowing us to discern them by our spiritual sense of *feel*. We have five natural senses and five spiritual senses. Concerning using these, the writer of Hebrews said,

> For though by this time you ought to be teachers, you need someone to teach you

again the first principles of the oracles of God; and you have come to need milk and not solid food. For everyone who partakes only of milk is unskilled in the word of righteousness, for he is a babe. But solid food belongs to those who are of full age, that is, those who *by reason of use have their senses exercised to discern both good and evil*. (Hebrews 5:12-14; italics mine)

In this passage of scripture, drinking milk and eating natural food is a parable. The milk symbolizes hearing and learning the word, and solid food symbolizes putting what you have learned into practice and actually doing the word. Peter said, "As newborn babes, desire the pure milk of the word, that you may grow thereby" (1 Peter 2:2). Likewise, when the disciples brought Jesus His lunch, He compared eating solid food to doing the Father's will:

But He said to them, "I have food to eat of which you do not know." Therefore, the disciples said to one another, "Has anyone brought Him anything to eat?" Jesus said to them, *"My food is to do the will of Him who sent Me, and to finish His work."* (John 4:34; italics mine)

The gift of discerning spirits is like walking into a dark room and feeling your way around. Sometimes it allows us to know the presence of angels or demons through the sense of smell, but, as we said above, it *primarily* operates through the spiritual sense of *feel*. Therefore, when angels appear, unless God allows us to see them with our spiritual sense of sight, we are in the dark. In that case, we must learn to feel our way around in the spirit realm, and then, by experience, learn to identify what we are feeling.

Notice in the scripture in Hebrews, quoted above, the writer implies the necessity of *learning* to use our spiritual senses. We must learn to be sensitive and ready to recognize and acknowledge what we are feeling and seeing because often these feelings are faint, and the visions are brief. Because of this, it is easy to miss what the Spirit is trying to show us. Paul even spoke of learning to prophecy! (See 1 Corinthians 14:31). Although some people are more gifted or naturally sensitive to the spiritual realm than others, we can all train ourselves to discern the presence of both angels and demons if we set our hearts to do so.

God is faithful. If we ask for Him, we have a wonderful Tutor available, called the Holy Spirit, whom the Father will send to personally teach and train every one of us. Jesus said,

> But the Helper, *the Holy Spirit, whom the Father will send in My name, He will teach you all things*, and bring to your remembrance all things that I said to you. (John 14:26; italics mine)

# Ask for the Angel

# Chapter Six

# The Angel of His Presence

In all their affliction He was afflicted, And *the Angel of His Presence* saved them; In His love and in His pity He redeemed them; And He bore them and carried them all the days of old. (Isaiah 63:9; italics mine)

As we mentioned in chapter 4, God is invisible, eternal, immortal, immutable, omnipotent, omniscient and omnipresent. Since He is invisible, He must use natural means to reveal His divine presence and supernatural attributes. Although He has revealed Himself in many ways in both His word and through His creation, He revealed Himself to Moses and Israel *through the Angel of*

*His Presence.* Several of His wonderful, supernatural attributes were manifest through this Angel. This is the same Angel who appeared to Moses in the burning bush. Likewise, He went before Israel, manifested as a cloud by day and a pillar of fire by night, as He led them through the wilderness to Canaan after they came out of Egypt. The first time Moses met Him was when he turned aside in the desert to see the bush that burned with fire but was not consumed. At this encounter, Moses called Him *"the Angel of the Lord"*.

> And the *Angel of the Lord* appeared to him in a flame of fire from the midst of a bush. So he looked, and behold, the bush was burning with fire, but the bush was not consumed... Moreover, He said, "I am the God of your father—the God of Abraham, the God of Isaac, and the God of Jacob." And Moses hid his face, for he was afraid to look upon God.

> And the Lord said: "I have surely seen the oppression of My people who are in Egypt, and have heard their cry because

of their taskmasters, for I know their sorrows. So I have come down to deliver them out of the hand of the Egyptians... Now therefore, behold, the cry of the children of Israel has come to Me, and I have also seen the oppression with which the Egyptians oppress them. Come now, therefore, and I will send you to Pharaoh that you may bring My people, the children of Israel, out of Egypt." But Moses said to God, "Who am I that I should go to Pharaoh, and that I should bring the children of Israel out of Egypt?" So, He said, *"I will certainly be with you..."* (Exodus 3:2, 6-12, italics mine)

Although there are many other passages of scripture that mention the angel of the Lord, one has to examine the context carefully to determine whether the scripture refers to the Lord Himself, or simply an angel sent by the Lord. In this instance, this Angel identifies Himself as the God of Moses' father, "the God of Abraham, the God of Isaac, and the God of Jacob", so, this Angel is an epiphany—a manifestation of God, Himself.

The fact that He promised Moses that He would certainly be with him also helps us tie the identity of this Angel with the one who led them through the wilderness. As we saw in the initial scripture that we introduced this chapter with, Isaiah called the Angel that went before Israel *the Angel of His Presence*!

There is one more thing that we need to know about Him. God told Moses to be careful to obey Him because His Name was in Him:

> Behold, I send an Angel before you to keep you in the way and to bring you into the place which I have prepared. Beware of Him and obey His voice; do not provoke Him, for He will not pardon your transgressions; *for My name is in Him*. But if you indeed obey His voice and do all that I speak, then I will be an enemy to your enemies and an adversary to your adversaries. (Exodus 23:20-22; italics mine)

Why is it important that we understand

who this Angel is? Because as He led Israel through the wilderness, He established a pattern and revealed a principle that we need to understand if we are going to work with God to fulfill His perfect will! Also, we must learn from Moses' failure and not make the same mistake that he made. Although the children of Israel followed Moses, Moses followed the Angel! When Moses took it upon himself to act other than the way the Angel instructed him to, he made a grievous error, and in doing so, forfeited his chance to enter the Promised Land. That is no small error! (See Numbers 20:10-12.)

As we read the following passage of scripture, remember that the cloud is the manifestation of the Angel of His Presence.

> Now on the day that the tabernacle was raised up, the cloud [Angel] covered the tabernacle, the tent of the Testimony; from evening until morning it was above the tabernacle like the appearance of fire. *So it was always: the cloud covered it by day, and the appearance of fire by night.* Whenever the cloud was taken up from

above the tabernacle, after that the children of Israel would journey; and in the place where the cloud settled, there the children of Israel would pitch their tents. *At the command of the Lord the children of Israel would journey, and at the command of the Lord they would camp; as long as the cloud stayed above the tabernacle they remained encamped. Even when the cloud continued long, many days above the tabernacle, the children of Israel kept the charge of the Lord and did not journey.* So it was, when the cloud was above the tabernacle a few days: according to the command of the Lord they would remain encamped, and according to the command of the Lord they would journey. (Numbers 9:15-20; italics mine)

Paul said, "For as many as are led by the Spirit of God, these are sons of God". (Romans 8:14). We are on a spiritual journey, and we are supposed to be led by the Spirit, and not just when we are in church on Sunday morning! If we are truly "sons of God", then our lives are not our own. That means that it is not up to us to decide what church we are supposed to be a member of, or what our ministry is supposed to be, or when or if we are supposed to move to a new location or change jobs to improve our circumstances—all these things, and much more, are supposed to be determined by God. We must think and live as bond-slaves of Christ. We are not of this world. We are citizens of the Kingdom of God! We cannot be a *light* to the world if we are *like* the world! We are called to be "a chosen generation, a royal priesthood, an holy nation, a peculiar people" (1 Peter 2:9). We cannot think and live the way this world does and still be the servants of Christ. Paul said,

> I beseech you therefore, brethren, by the mercies of God, that you *present your bodies a living sacrifice,* holy, acceptable to God, which is your reasonable service. *And do not be conformed to this world,* but be transformed by the renewing of your mind, that you may prove what is that good and acceptable and perfect will of God. (Romans 12:1-2; italics mine)

If we conform to this world's way of thinking and doing things, we will become Laodiceans and not even know it! (See Revelation 3:14-22.) Laodicean means "the people's choice". Laodiceans are those who call themselves Christians, but they are Christian in name only. This is the end-times church that thinks they have it all together, but Christ said they are wretched and totally depraved. Concerning them, Jesus said that although they say they are rich and have need of nothing, but they are so far from God that they are completely unconscious of the fact that they are wretched, miserable, poor, blind, and naked. Because they are lukewarm, He is going to vomit them out of His mouth!

Is there hope for them (or us, if we also become deceived and grow distant and lukewarm)? The answer is yes, there is, but only if they come to their senses and sincerely repent! Jesus followed His severe rebuke of them with these instructions:

> I counsel you to buy from Me gold refined in the fire, that you may be rich;

and white garments, that you may be clothed, that the shame of your nakedness may not be revealed; and anoint your eyes with eye salve, that you may see. (Revelation 3:18)

Today's traditional church is blind to many things, including their own condition before the Lord. If we seek God for the Holy Spirit and allow Him to teach us to discern spiritual things, we are taking a giant step in the right direction. We must acknowledge Him in all our ways and listen for His corrections and directions to get back on the right track. As Isaiah said, the Angel of His Presence will save us from this present evil world and lead us to victory if we faithfully follow His wise leadership.

# Ask for the Angel

# Chapter Seven

## Messenger Angels

The Hebrew word *malak*, from the Old Testament and the Greek word *angelos* from the New Testament are both translated by the English word *angel* in the English translations of the Bible. Both words have the same literal meaning—*messenger*. Although, in almost all cases, both are translated angel, in a few instances the more literal meaning is the more correct rendering. Although many of God's holy angels are messengers, not all of them are. We will study the great variety of angels in the next chapter, but now we will examine the way God's messenger angels minister to us.

There are only two angels whose names are

given in the Protestant Bible—Gabriel and Michael. Gabriel is obviously a messenger, but Michael is a warrior. Gabriel said that Michael was a "chief prince", and Jude called him an archangel (see Daniel 10:13, 12:1; Revelation 12:7; Jude 1:9). Judging by the importance of the messages Gabriel delivers, he also appears to be a high-ranking angel, although he is not called an archangel in Scripture. Both Michael and Gabriel are mentioned in both the Old and New Testaments.

There is another angel who is named but not in the Protestant canon of Scripture—Raphael. His name means *"God has healed"* and his name is found in the book of Tobit (in the Apocrypha) and in 1 Enoch (considered by some as one of the lost books of the Bible). The ancient rabbis believed that Raphael was the angel that healed the people at the pool of Bethesda, which we discussed in chapter 3. Another angel's name that is not in the Bible but is recognized in the Anglican Church and certain Christian traditions is Uriel (or Auriel), who is considered the angel of prophecy and wisdom. In Hebrew, his name means "God is my flame".

## Messenger Angels

Gabriel is first introduced to us by Daniel, where the angel responds to his request to understand a vision that he received about the rise and fall of nations. His second appearance is in response to Daniel's 21 day fast. He doesn't show up again until several hundred years later when he is sent to tell the priest Zacharias that his wife was going to conceive and bear a son, whom he was to name John. Six months later he appeared to Mary and informed her that she was chosen to bring forth a Son, whom she was to name Jesus—the long-awaited Messiah. (see Daniel 8:16, 9:21; Luke 1:19, 26)

Gabriel doesn't appear by name again in the Scriptures, but obviously, he is still faithfully going about the Father's business of delivering messages to whomever he is sent. Perhaps he has even been sent to speak to you and has shown you something. When? While you were asleep, in your dreams.

Quite often people are visited by angels in their dreams, but the angels seldom make their presence known to them, so, they don't realize that it was an angel that spoke to them. Angels are sent to both believers and non-believers, alike. In recent years many Muslims have been converted to Christianity because of angelic visitations in their dreams.

Biblical angels sometimes appear in bright clothing or have a fierce countenance. This is to identify them so that those who see them will recognize that they are the Lord's messengers. In our dreams, the opposite approach is usually taken. They are there, informing us of things to come, or showing us things that we need to know, but when we are awakened, we can't describe them. The reason? By remaining anonymous the emphasis is always on the message rather than the messenger.

The Scriptures abound with stories of angels speaking to people in their dreams. Jacob was dreaming when he saw the angels ascending and descending on the ladder that reached into heaven. Later, an angel gave him a dream telling him that it was time for him to leave his father-in-law's employment and return to the land of his kindred. (see Genesis 31:11-13). In the New Testament, an angel

## Messenger Angels

visited Joseph in his dreams five different times; first to tell him to marry Mary, then to tell him how to protect the Child that he was entrusted to raise. (see Matthew 1:18-21, 2:12-14, 2:19-22)

Angels may also appear to us in visions while we are awake, as one did to Philip when he sent him into the desert to meet the high-ranking Ethiopian eunuch that needed someone to explain the Scriptures to him.

> Now an angel of the Lord spoke to Philip, saying, "Arise and go toward the south along the road which goes down from Jerusalem to Gaza." This is desert. So he arose and went. And behold, a man of Ethiopia, a eunuch of great authority under Candace the queen of the Ethiopians, who had charge of all her treasury, and had come to Jerusalem to worship, was returning. And sitting in his chariot, he was reading Isaiah the prophet. Then the Spirit said to Philip, "Go near and overtake this chariot." So, Philip ran to him, and heard him reading

the prophet Isaiah, and said, "Do you understand what you are reading?" And he said, "How can I, unless someone guides me?" And he asked Philip to come up and sit with him. (Acts 8:26-31)

Another way angels may appear to us is in night visions (a night vision is a dream where there is a tangible anointing present. Because of the anointing, there is no question that the dream or vision is from God).

And a vision appeared to Paul in the night. A man [*angel*] of Macedonia stood and pleaded with him, saying, "Come over to Macedonia and help us." Now after he had seen the vision, immediately we sought to go to Macedonia, concluding that the Lord had called us to preach the gospel to them. (Acts 16:9-10)

We know the "man" in Paul's vision was an angel because when they got to Macedonia, it wasn't a man whom they met and helped, it was Lydia, a godly woman who was leading a prayer meeting!

## Messenger Angels

God often sends angels to His ministers, while they are asleep, to give them the message that He wants them to deliver to His people. John was shown such an angel (although he wasn't asleep at the time):

> Then I saw another angel flying in the midst of heaven, having the everlasting gospel to preach to those who dwell on the earth—to every nation, tribe, tongue, and people— saying with a loud voice, *"Fear God and give glory to Him, for the hour of His judgment has come; and worship Him who made heaven and earth, the sea and springs of water."* (Revelation 14:6-7; italics mine)

There are times when it takes more than just asking God for angels before we can get their help. Sometimes we are required to make a sacrifice before God will send them to minister to our needs. God's blessings often require sacrifice and the greater the blessing, the greater the sacrifice needs to be. For example, the greatest blessing of all is eternal life and it required the greatest sacrifice of all; the sacrifice of God's only begotten Son!

Paul said that Abraham is the father of faith, and that we should walk in his footsteps. When Abraham wanted to hear from God, he built an altar and offered a sacrifice. We should follow his example. In our culture, the suggestion to offer a sacrifice often implies making a significant financial contribution, which not everyone can afford. But fasting is a sacrifice that everyone can make, both rich and poor alike. Also, the Bible gives us some wonderful promises that are available to us through fasting. (see Genesis 12:8; Romans 4:12)

Isaiah gives us detailed instructions on offering an acceptable fast to the Lord and the amazing benefits that we can expect when we fast properly. (see Isaiah 58:1-14). One especially important promise that Isaiah gave concerns our nation's Christian foundation. Our nation was founded on godly principles by God fearing men. It has been drifting away from its anchor for several generations now. As a nation, we are far from the godly foundation that our forefathers fought and died to establish and provide for us. David asked, "If the foundations are destroyed, what can the righteous do?". (Psalm 11:3). But if we fast, Isaiah said,

> Those from among you Shall build the old waste places; *You shall raise up the foundations of many generations*; And you shall be called the Repairer of the Breach, The Restorer of Streets [*or paths*] to Dwell In. (Isaiah 58:12; italics mine)

What criteria does God use to determine if a fast is acceptable or not? He primarily judges our motives. Why and what are we fasting for? If we fast to persuade God to hear our prayers and do our will instead of fasting to subdue our fleshly desires and hear His voice, He doesn't accept our fast. But, if during your fast, you set your heart to, "...honor Him, not doing your own ways, Nor finding your own pleasure, Nor speaking your own words, *Then you shall delight yourself in the Lord...*" (Isaiah 58:13-14; italics mine).

When Paul was on his way to Rome a raging typhoon named Euroclydon wrecked the ship he was on. In their struggles to keep the ship afloat, the sailors threw everything that wasn't nailed down overboard and declared a fast, and after long abstinence, when everything appeared to be utterly hopeless, an angel appeared to Paul with a very encouraging message!

> And now I urge you to take heart, for there will be no loss of life among you, but only of the ship. For there stood by me this night an angel of the God to whom I belong and whom I serve, saying, "Do not be afraid, Paul; you must be brought before Caesar; and indeed, God has granted you [*the lives*] all those who sail with you". (See Acts 27:14-24)

God's messengers and messages take many forms and serve many purposes. Some warn us of impending danger. Some help us make important, difficult decisions and instruct us what to do or say in certain circumstances. Others encourage and help us persevere through difficult times, as in Paul's case above.

## Messenger Angels

All His messages are invaluable and life giving.

God's word, whether written in the Bible or spoken by His angels, are given to impart and sustain life in those who are receptive to them. If we desire to prosper and walk in the fullness of the blessings of gospel of Christ, we should ask for the angels and hearken to the messages they deliver. Sometimes even our life may depend upon it!

# Ask for the Angel

# Chapter Eight

## Asking Specifically

### Guardian Angels

Although Psalm 91 is one of the most popular and often quoted Psalms in the Bible, few people pay attention to the fact that, in addition to the necessity of asking for its fulfillment (as we discussed in the first chapter), several conditions that are necessary for its fulfilment are actually contained within the Psalm, itself!

*He who dwells in the secret place of the Most High Shall abide under the shadow of the Almighty ...Because you have made the Lord, who is my refuge, Even the Most High, your dwelling place,* No evil shall befall you, Nor shall any plague come near your dwelling; *For He shall give His angels charge over you, To keep you in all your ways.* In their hands they shall bear you up, Lest you dash your foot against a stone.... *Because he has set his love upon Me,* therefore I will deliver him; I will set him on high, because he has known My name. *He shall call upon Me, and I will answer him*; I will be with him in trouble; *I will deliver him* and honor him. With long life I will satisfy him, And show him My salvation." (Psalm 91:1, 9-12, 14-16; italics mine)

This beloved Psalm starts out with *"He who dwells in the secret place of the Most High"*. Sad to say, not everyone who can quote this Psalm can legitimately claim to dwell there. In fact, many Christians don't even know what or where the secret place of the Most High is!

The second condition is a continuation of the first: *"Because you have made the Lord... your dwelling places"*. Jesus said, "If you abide in Me, and My words abide in you, you will ask what you desire, and it shall be done for you" (John 15:7). So, before we can ask for the fulfillment of the manifold blessings and benefits of this Psalm and expect to receive the ministry of the angels (who carry out and perform its wonderful, precious promises), we have to surrender our lives wholly unto God and learn to live in His presence.

The third condition is, *"Because he has set his love upon Me"*. This is especially relevant for us today because Jesus warned us that in the latter days, when His return is imminent, that lawlessness will abound and the love of many will grow cold (see Matthew 24:12). In the fast-paced, materialistic society that we live in today, it is easy to become distracted and drawn away from our first love. We must deliberately take time to stroke the embers of our devotion for the Lord through daily prayer and worship, and by reading and meditating upon His word. Otherwise, our hearts will become calloused and like the infamous frog in the teakettle, we will gradually be overcome by "the cares of this world, the deceitfulness of riches, and the desires for other things", causing us to become cold and distant in our relationship with God (see Mark 4:19).

Daniel is a biblical character who continually dwelt in "the secret place of the Most High". He never allowed the pressures of public service, nor the pleasures readily available to him by reason of his close association with royalty, to distract him from daily spending time with God through prayer and meditation on His word. The morning after he was thrown into the lion's den for refusing to obey the king's edict to cease praying to any god but himself, Daniel testified to the king,

> My God sent His angel and shut the lions' mouths, so that they have not hurt me, because I was found innocent before Him; and also, O king, I have done no wrong before you. (Daniel 6:22)

We should continually strive to meet His conditions and in our daily prayers, ask for both angelic protection and provision, especially as we travel. If we travel away from home, we should ask for angelic protection as we go and angels to take care of our family's needs while we are away. The latter part of this passage from Psalm 91, quoted above, introduces our next classification of angels—angels that have the power to deliver us from both demons and adverse circumstance!

## Angels of Deliverance

Another angel that we should ask for as we strive to obey the Lord and freely minister to others is the angel of deliverance. Ministering deliverance is not hard, but it is far too complex and involved to teach in just a few short paragraphs. So, the following brief introduction and discourse concerning deliverance is quite limited in its scope. Nevertheless, there are several important things that we need to know before attempting deliverance. Jesus introduced two of these in the following parable,

> But if I cast out demons *with the finger of God*, surely the kingdom of God has come upon you. When a strong man, fully armed, guards his own palace, his goods are in peace. But when a stronger than he comes upon him and overcomes

him, *he takes from him all his armor in which he trusted,* and divides his spoils. (Luke 11:20-22; italics mine)

The first thing in this passage of scripture that we should take note of is *the finger of God.* God's finger is the convicting power of the Holy Spirit, or, in some cases, His fingers refer directly to His angels. (See Exodus 8:16-19; 31:18; Galatians 3:19.) We need both! We should always ask for both Holy Spirit and angelic assistance before attempting to set someone free from demons. Next, we should take the demon's armor that he is trusting in away from him. Otherwise, he will come back and reoccupy his former dwelling, and Jesus said the victim would then be in worse condition than he was before he was ministered to! (See Luke 11:26.)

Although traumatic experiences may enable demons to enter and torment people with bad dreams or various and sundry phobias, such as claustrophobia and aquaphobia, *the primary armor that demons use to hold their victims in bondage is sin:*

## Asking Specifically

> Jesus answered them, "Most assuredly, I say to you, whoever commits sin is a slave of sin... Therefore, if the Son makes you free, you shall be free indeed." (John 8:34, 36)

*Whoever commits sin is a slave of sin!* Jesus assured us that sin authorizes demons to enslave their victims, and before he or she can obtain lasting freedom, the sin must be exposed and removed through confession and faith in Christ's redeeming blood. John assured us that if we would confess, God would forgive!

> If we confess our sins, He is faithful and just to forgive us our sins and to cleanse us from all unrighteousness. (1 John 1:9).

Sometimes it is the victim's own personal sin that must be confessed and sometimes it is someone else's trespass against the victim that has armed the demon. In the case of the victim's own sin, as stated above, it must be forgiven through confession and faith in Christ's blood. In the case of a trespass against the victim, *as an act of his or her will*, both the trespasser and the trespass must be forgiven. It is important to understand that forgiveness is not a feeling, it is a choice. If we sincerely choose to forgive, regardless of how we feel about the matter, we will be set free from the offense. Otherwise, we will remain in bondage.

How can we tell if someone needs deliverance? Demons manifest themselves in different ways through different people, but demonized people usually exhibit one or more (but certainly not all) of the following behavioral characteristics: Some demonized people are overly impulsive or compulsive, or may exhibit obsessive, uncontrollable behavior. Those operating in witchcraft are usually possessive, exhibiting manipulative and controlling behavior, while other demons may cause people to be cruel and hateful (and these people are often angry and profane). Also, people who are habitually rebellious and disobedient toward legitimate and proper authorities are yielding to demons.

Another demonic trait is slothfulness (which is often accompanied by waste-fulness). Like all demons, this one can be quite

## Asking Specifically

deceiving. His victims may work hard to earn material things and at the same time be slothful and negligent in the more important, spiritual things that God told us to seek after!

Phobias and addictive behaviors, including both psychological and chemical addictions, such as alcohol and smoking, are caused by demons. Psychological addictions may include eating disorders, such as bulimia and anorexia, or addictions such as gambling or various fetishes. Likewise, all sexual sin, such as adultery, promiscuity, pedophilia, pornography and voyeurism, these are all demonically motivated. Another, less known and often overlooked aspect of demonization in some people, especially in those who have been sexually molested in their youth, is frigidity. A demon that can inflame an emotion can also suppress that same emotion when it is in his best interest to do so.

This list is not exhaustive, but these are some of the more common manifestations that we have encountered over the years as we have ministered to God's people. And lastly, our experience has shown that both believers and nonbelievers, alike, may possess demons and need deliverance.

There is another type of deliverance in which holy angels excel—deliverance from difficult, adverse circumstances. Besides those we noted in Psalm 91, David gives us an insight into another important condition that God's promises of deliverance and protection are predicated upon—we must walk in the fear of the Lord:

> This poor man cried out, and the Lord heard him, and saved him out of all his troubles. The angel of the Lord encamps all around those who fear Him, and delivers them. (2. Psalm 34:6-7)

Jesus said, "And do not fear those who kill the body but cannot kill the soul. But rather fear Him who is able to destroy both soul and body in hell" (Matthew 10:28). The biblical story of the three Hebrew children who willfully disobeyed the king's command perfectly illustrates putting this principle to work. When confronted and threatened to be thrown into a fiery furnace for their refusal to bow before a golden image that King Nebuchadnezzar had set up, they fearlessly replied:

> Shadrach, Meshach, and Abed-Nego answered and said to the king... "we have no need to answer you in this matter. If that is the case, our God whom we serve is able to deliver us from the burning fiery furnace, and He will deliver us from your hand, O king. But if not, let it be known to you, O king, that we do not serve your gods, nor will we worship the gold image which you have set up." (Daniel 3:16-18)

Of course, the outraged king instantly reacted to their disobedience, which he (mistakenly) perceived as rebellion and intolerable insolence:

> Then Nebuchadnezzar was full of fury, and the expression on his face changed toward Shadrach, Meshach, and Abed-Nego... And he commanded certain mighty men of valor who were in his army to bind Shadrach, Meshach, and

Abed-Nego, and cast them into the burning fiery furnace... And these three men, Shadrach, Meshach, and Abed-Nego, fell down bound into the midst of the burning fiery furnace. Then King Nebuchadnezzar was astonished; and he rose in haste and spoke, saying to his counselors, "Did we not cast three men bound into the midst of the fire?" They answered and said to the king, "True, O king." "Look!" he answered, "I see four men loose, walking in the midst of the fire; and they are not hurt, and the form of the fourth is like the Son of God." (Daniel 3:19-25)

Once Nebuchadnezzar saw the fourth Man in the furnace, he realized his mistake!

Nebuchadnezzar spoke, saying, "Blessed be the God of Shadrach, Meshach, and Abed-Nego, *who sent His Angel and delivered His servants who trusted in Him, and they have frustrated the king's word*, and yielded their bodies, that they should not serve nor worship any god except their own God! Therefore, I make a decree that any people, nation, or language which speaks anything amiss against the God of Shadrach, Meshach, and Abed-Nego shall be cut in pieces, and their houses shall be made an ash heap; *because there is no other God who can deliver like this."* (Daniel 3:28-29; italics mine)

Jacob was a trouble magnet, always getting himself into tight spots, but God had a purpose in Jacob, so, He took good care of him, anyway. Right before Jacob died, he blessed Joseph's two boys. During this simple ceremony, he acknowledged the Angel of the Lord's lifelong protection and deliverance over his life and decreed the same blessing over his two grandsons. He prayed, "The Angel who has redeemed me from all evil, bless the lads". (Genesis 48:16)

Peter was another impulsive man who was prone to get into serious trouble, and sometimes needed angelic deliverance! In Acts, Luke gives us a detailed account of Peter's miraculous deliverance from prison after Herod had him arrested:

> Peter was therefore kept in prison, but constant prayer was offered to God for him by the church. And when Herod was about to bring him out, that night Peter was sleeping, bound with two chains between two soldiers; and the guards before the door were keeping the prison. Now behold, an angel of the Lord stood by him, and a light shone in the prison; and he struck Peter on the side and raised him up, saying, "Arise quickly!" And his chains fell off his hands. Then the angel said to him, "Gird yourself and tie on your sandals"; and so he did. And he said to him, "Put on your garment and follow me." So he went out and followed him, and did not know that what was done by the angel was real, but thought he was seeing a vision. When they were past the first and the second guard posts, they came to the iron gate that leads to the city, which opened to them of its own accord; and

they went out and went down one street, and immediately the angel departed from him. And when Peter had come to himself, he said, "Now I know for certain that the Lord has sent His angel and has delivered me from the hand of Herod and from all the expectation of the Jewish people." (Acts 12:5-11)

Before Peter was imprisoned, James was arrested and subsequently executed. There is no record that the church prayed for him during his confinement. They apparently took God's protection for granted, which was and is a grievous mistake! James lost his life before the church awakened to the necessity of prayer! The Kingdom of God is not just voice activated, it is prayer activated, too! When the church prayed, God dispatched an angel to open the prison doors and set Peter free.

Although, many of us may never suffer being put into prison, that is not the only adverse circumstance that we may encounter in life. Regardless of the specific warfare or difficulty that we are confronted with, or whatever our need may be, we should make it known to God through supplication and fasting, and while praying, we should ask God to send the specific angel who is equipped to minister to our specific need.

## Breakthrough Angels

Angels are instrumental in enabling the Father's elect to achieve His will, and one such angel that we haven't mentioned before is a *breakthrough* angel. These angels work together with the angels of deliverance, discussed above. Without a doubt, these powerful angels are the ones who enabled the three mighty men from David's troop to defy the odds and break though the Philistine host to bring him a drink from the well of Bethlehem:

> Now three of the thirty chief men went down to the rock to David, into the cave of Adullam; and the army of the Philistines encamped in the Valley of Rephaim. David was then in the stronghold, and the garrison of the Philistines was then in Bethlehem. And David said with longing, "Oh, that

someone would give me a drink of water from the well of Bethlehem, which is by the gate!" *So the three broke through the camp of the Philistines,* drew water from the well of Bethlehem that was by the gate, and took it and brought it to David. Nevertheless, David would not drink it, but poured it out to the Lord. (1 Chronicles 11:15-18; italics mine)

Immediately after David was crowned king over all Israel, the Philistines gathered an army against him and invaded the Valley of Rephaim. After he defeated them there, "David said, 'God has broken through my enemies by my hand like a breakthrough of water.' Therefore, they called the name of that place Baal Perazim". (meaning *master* or *lord of breakthrough*—1 Chronicles 14:8-11)

We are all faced with extremely burdensome and seemingly impossible tasks at one time or another. It is comforting to know that God has prepared specific angels equipped to give us the necessary breakthrough when every other avenue of success or deliverance appears blocked. These powerful angels are like all the others, they are not far away and hard to get—they are instant in response to our cry for help! God is faithful. If we ask in faith, believing, He has prepared the answers even before the problems arise!

In the process of praying for angelic help, or for anything else that we may ask for, if we ask for and receive the aid of the next angel that we introduce, our prayers will dramatically increase in their effectiveness!

## The Angel of Supplication

If there is an angel more important than all the others, yet one that is the least acknowledged and asked for, it is probably the angel that enables us to prevail in prayer—the angel of Supplication (or Intercession). Immediately before Jesus returns and makes Himself known to His Jewish brethren, He will pour out the *"Spirit of grace and supplication"* upon the whole nation of Israel (see Zechariah 12:10; Isaiah 66:8). This is the angel that strengthened Jesus as He prayed in the Garden, right before He was arrested:

## Asking Specifically

And [*Jesus*] was withdrawn from them about a stone's throw, and He knelt down and prayed, saying, "Father, if it is Your will, take this cup away from Me; nevertheless, not My will, but Yours, be done." *Then an angel appeared to Him from heaven, strengthening Him. And being in agony, He prayed more earnestly.* Then His sweat became like great drops of blood falling down to the ground. (Luke 22:41-44; italics mine)

The word that best describes this powerful angel's manifestation is the word *travail*. The effectiveness of his ministry is seen in Isaiah's description of Jesus' sacrificial offering of Himself for our sins:

*He shall see of the travail of his soul,* and shall be satisfied: by his knowledge shall my righteous servant justify many; for he shall bear their iniquities. (Isaiah 53:11; KJV, italics mine)

This angel not only strengthened Jesus in prayer, enabling Him to overcome the ordeal of the cross, He enabled Paul to bring whole regions under the sway of the gospel. When writing to the Galatians, Paul describes the travailing prayer and deep concern that he has for them because of the deceptive, legalistic heresy they have fallen into, which was perverting the gospel that he had previously delivered to them:

> My little children, of whom I travail in birth again until Christ be formed in you. (Galatians 4:19; KJV)

Women travail in birth to bring forth natural sons and Zion must do the same to bring forth her spiritual sons! (See Psalm 87:5-6.) We should invite this angel's assistance into every prayer session that we attend.

## Angels of Prosperity

The biblical meaning of prosperity is not exactly the same as the secular meaning. The primary, secular meaning of prosperity is "economic well-being". Biblical prosperity includes financial provision when and where it is needed but it is not limited to the financial realm. In his third letter to the church, John prayed,

> Beloved, I pray that you may prosper in all things and be in health, just as your soul prospers. (3 John 1:2)

John's prayer for prosperity covered "all things", not just finances. The Greek word *euodoo* that he used, translated *prosper,* means *"to have a good journey"*. A good journey includes having enough finances to cover our needs, but being broke down in the middle of Death Valley with a trunk full of money could hardly be called prospering! Money is important, but only in the sense that it is needed to satisfy certain needs. There are far more important things in life than money and we should focus our attention on them, not on the temporary things this world has to offer. We should especially seek those things that are above. Things that "endure to eternal life", as Jesus admonished us to do. He said,

> Do not labor for the food which perishes, but for the food which endures to everlasting life, which the Son of Man will give you, because God the Father

has set His seal on Him. (John 6:27)

When Abraham sent his servant to get a wife for his son Isaac, he told him that God would send the angel of prosperity before him to give him success. When he arrived at Laban's house (Isaac's future brother-in-law), the servant repeated what Abraham had told him,

> But [*Abraham*] said to me, 'The Lord, before whom I walk, will send His angel with you and prosper your way; and you shall take a wife for my son from my family and from my father's house. (Gen. 24:40)

Perhaps he would go and get a spouse for your son or daughter, too, if you asked God for his assistance. Also, he is not limited to matchmaking. As John said, we need to prosper in health and happiness, too! (Although perhaps we should point out that both science and the Scriptures teach that both good health and lasting peace and happiness are often directly related to whether we have a good marriage or not!)

## The Angel of Healing

Although we introduced the angel of healing in chapter 3, as a reminder, we will briefly examine his ministry here. Although the Scriptures often reveal *what* God does, they don't always give us a behind-the-scenes look at *how* it is done. But since we know that "angels do His word", when someone speaks and miracles are performed, we can safely assume that angels performed the miracle. For example, when Paul discerned that a certain lame man believed the word that he was preaching about Jesus's blood atoning for both our sins and our sicknesses, he commanded the man to stand up and he instantly obeyed:

> And in Lystra a certain man without strength in his feet was sitting, a cripple from his mother's womb, who had never walked. This man heard Paul speaking. Paul, observing him intently and seeing that he had faith to be healed, said with a loud voice, "Stand up straight on your feet!" And he leaped and walked. (Acts 14:8-10)

As we can see from this example, like all the others, healing angels are readily available if we exercise our faith. Nevertheless, in our society many Christians turn to doctors and medicine instead of first seeking God and asking Him to heal them. In the process, they rob God of the glory and themselves of the blessing!

> For the hearts of this people have grown dull. Their ears are hard of hearing, And their eyes they have closed, Lest they should see with their eyes and hear with their ears, Lest they should understand with their hearts and turn, So that I should heal them. (Acts 28:27)

David said that God was the One "Who forgives all your iniquities, Who heals all your diseases" (Psalm 103:3). God's promise of "healing all your diseases" is like every other promise; we have to ask in faith to receive its benefits, and as the scripture above shows, faith comes by hearing!

## Angels of Provision

We briefly discussed angels of provision in chapter 4, where we saw that an angel fed Elijah twice when he was exhausted after fleeing from Jezebel. Not surprisingly, God also used angels to feed the children of Israel manna when they wandered for forty years in the wilderness. The Psalmist said that God,

> Had rained down manna on them to eat, and given them of the bread of heaven. Men ate angels' food; He sent them food to the full. (Psalm 78:24-25)

Since we know that angels "do His word", we should realize that angels are constantly active in our lives, even though we may not see them. Even when we cannot discern them, their works betray their presence. For example, when Jesus told Peter to go fishing to get the temple-tax money, obviously, it was an angel who put the money in the fish's mouth and caused him to bite Peter's hook!

> When they had come to Capernaum, those who received the temple tax came

to Peter and said, "Does your Teacher not pay the temple tax?" He said, "Yes."... [*then Jesus said,*] "Nevertheless, lest we offend them, go to the sea, cast in a hook, and take the fish that comes up first. And when you have opened its mouth, you will find a piece of money; take that and give it to them for Me and you." (See Matthew 17:24-27)

Some angels are incredibly powerful and have amazing, supernatural abilities, even exercising power over nature, itself! When the disciples were in a large rowboat and a violent storm arose, they were in danger of sinking. They awakened Jesus and He arose and stood in the bow of the boat and rebuked the wind and spoke to the sea, and the raging wind instantly ceased, and the waves became calm! (See Mark 4:36-39.) The endangered disciples were astonished!

> And they feared exceedingly, and said to one another, "Who can this be, that even the wind and the sea obey Him!" (Mark 4:41)

## Asking Specifically

Strong's Concordance defines the Greek word *hypakouo*, translated *obey*, in the verse above as, *"to hear under (as a subordinate), i.e., to listen attentively"*. The ever-present angels heard His command and acted accordingly. They were invisible to the undiscerning disciples who only saw their works, so, they attributed the miracle to the wind and the sea — thinking that the wind and sea, of their own accord, could hear and hearken to His command.

History records several miracles of nature that helped George Washington during the American Revolution. In one instance, in the early stages of the war, in the aftermath of losing one battle a timely, unexpected and unexplainable fog appeared along a riverbank, in an area that almost never has fog, that hid his troops and enabled them to retreat and escape from the British. Washington called it "providence", but it was a clear sign that God was working to establish this nation for His own purposes.

If His saints will earnestly fast and pray, He

will still send his angels to work and fight for us! He promised that He would "restore the foundations of many generations" in response to our fasting! We should never give up in despair regardless of what we see happening in our country because of governmental corruption and incompetence. All of God's promises are yes and amen!

> If My people who are called by My name will humble themselves [*by fasting*], and pray and seek My face, and turn from their wicked ways, then I will hear from heaven, and will forgive their sin and heal their land. (2 Chronicles 7:14; also see Psalm 35:13)

Nothing is impossible with God! Whether it is supplying food for Elijah and the widow woman who sustained him during the famine that Elijah's own prayers had brought upon the land, or multiplying a few loaves and fish to feed five thousand hungry men—the angels work tirelessly to perform God's word and meet His children's needs. We need only ask.

Asking Specifically

# The Angel of Wisdom

If gold was available just for the asking, there would be a long line of excited people patiently waiting with their hands out, hoping to get their share. But Solomon said that wisdom was far more valuable than gold, and he should know because he had an abundance of both!

> *How much better to get wisdom than gold!* And to get understanding is to be chosen rather than silver [*and*] *Happy is the man who finds wisdom*, And the man who gains understanding; For her proceeds are better than the profits of silver, And her gain than fine gold. She is more precious than rubies, And all the things you may desire cannot compare with her. *Length of days is in her right hand,* In her left-hand riches and honor. Her ways are ways of pleasantness, And all her paths are peace. *She is a tree of life to those who take hold of her*, And happy are all who retain her. (Proverbs 16:16; 3:13-18; italics mine)

Solomon spoke of *finding* wisdom, but James said that it was free for the asking, and you don't even have to stand in line to get it! All you have to do is ask!

> If any of you lacks wisdom, let him ask of God, who gives to all liberally and without reproach, and it will be given to him. (James 1:5)

Paul also spoke of praying for wisdom. In fact, he prayed for the Ephesians to be filled with the spirit of wisdom and revelation in the knowledge of Christ (see Ephesians 1:16-17). Although the *"spirit of wisdom"* is one of the seven Spirits of God, there is also an *angel* of wisdom. (Since God reveals Himself both *to* and *through* His creation, and angels are part of His creation, it is possible, and even likely, that the seven Spirits of God are seven categories of angels—see Isaiah 11:1-4).

David knew the angel of wisdom even before Solomon was introduced to him. When Joab tried to outwit David, with the aid of the angel, David discerned his deviousness,

To bring about this change of affairs your servant Joab has done this thing; but my lord [*King David*] is wise, according to the wisdom of the angel of God, to know everything that is in the earth." (2 Samuel 14:18-20)

Wisdom is the ability to acquire knowledge and use it appropriately and in a timely fashion. Wisdom, combined with full, complete and insightful knowledge, gives one "the full assurance of understanding'. (Proverbs 3:19, 24:2, 8:12; Colossians 2:2-3; Ecclesiastes 10:10). The gift of a word of wisdom is a wonderful gift, but the angel of wisdom working through and alongside of you is far better! It behooves us to ask God to give us this angel as a life-long assistant.

## The Angel of Adversity (or Chastisement)

One of the most interesting encounters between man and angels in the whole Bible is found in the book of Numbers. This story also shows us that sometimes animals are much more sensitive to the spiritual realm than humans are. It is the story of a man who was so set on having his own way that he argues with a talking donkey! Because the story is quite long, I have omitted a few parts for the sake of brevity.

> Then God's anger was aroused because [*Balaam*] went, [*even though He had previously been told not to*] and *the Angel of the Lord took His stand in the way as an adversary against him*... Now the donkey saw the Angel of the Lord standing in the way with His drawn sword in His hand, and the donkey turned aside out of the way... Balaam struck the donkey to turn her back onto the road. Then the Angel of the Lord stood in a narrow path between the vineyards, with a wall on this side and a wall on that side. And when the donkey saw the Angel of the Lord, she pushed herself against the wall and crushed Balaam's foot against the wall; so he struck her again. Then the Angel of the Lord went..., and stood in a narrow place where there was no way to turn either to the right hand or to the left. And when the donkey saw the Angel of

## Asking Specifically

the Lord, she lay down under Balaam; so Balaam's anger was aroused, and he struck the donkey with his staff.

Then the Lord opened the mouth of the donkey, and she said to Balaam, "What have I done to you, that you have struck me these three times?" And Balaam said to the donkey, "Because you have abused me. I wish there were a sword in my hand, for now I would kill you!"... Then the Lord opened Balaam's eyes, and he saw the Angel of the Lord standing in the way with His drawn sword in His hand; and he bowed his head and fell flat on his face. And the Angel of the Lord said to him,... *"Behold, I have come out to stand against you, because your way is perverse before Me...* If she had not turned aside from Me, surely, I would also have killed you by now, and let her live." (Numbers 22:22-33; italics mine)

Sometimes we think the devil is withstanding us when in reality it is the Lord,

Himself, standing in our way! Solomon said, "In the day of prosperity be joyful, but in the day of adversity consider..." (Ecclesiastes 7:14). Why consider? Because things may not be as they appear. God may be talking to you through your adverse circumstances. Sometimes adversity is the only way He can get our attention!

## The Angel of Encouragement

Although we examined the following passage of scripture in chapter 7, I have reintroduced it here as a reminder that when the need arises, this angel is available, if we ask for him. Perhaps we should ask, not only for ourselves, but for God to also send him to comfort and encourage our neighbor when he or she is discouraged.

> And now I urge you to take heart, for there will be no loss of life among you, but only of the ship. For there stood by me this night an angel of the God to whom I belong and whom I serve, saying, 'Do not be afraid, Paul; you must be brought before Caesar; and indeed,

God has granted you [*the life of*] all those who sail with you.' (Acts 27:22-24; also see Acts 28:1-9)

The fact that the angel told Paul that God had granted him all those who sailed with him indicates that he had been praying, not only for his own life, but for the life of the sailors as well. It is also quite possible that they were all converted to Christianity during their ordeal, especially after they were stranded upon the island and saw the miraculous signs and wonders that God performed through Paul's hands.

## Harvest Angels

These next two angels sometimes work as a team. Each one has a specific role to fulfill. Harvest angels are those who reap the harvest fields to bring in the lost as well as those who administer God's judgments upon the wicked who reject God's counsel and refuse to repent of their ungodly deeds. After Jesus told the disciples the parable of the wheat and tares, He explained who the players were,

He answered and said to them: "He who sows the good seed is the Son of Man. The field is the world, the good seeds are the sons of the kingdom, but the tares are the sons of the wicked one. The enemy who sowed them is the devil, *the harvest is the end of the age, and the reapers are the angels*... The Son of Man will send out His angels, and they will gather out of His kingdom all things that offend, and those who practice lawlessness." (See Matthew 13:24-41; italics mine)

In His explanation, Jesus identified the angels who gather *in* the good seed and those who separate *out* the bad, offensive seed. The angels who gather in the good seed are those who are active in the last, end-time revival that brings in and saves the final harvest of souls that James said that God is patiently waiting for,

> Therefore, be patient, brethren, until the coming of the Lord. See how the farmer waits for the precious fruit of the earth, waiting patiently for it until it receives

## Asking Specifically

the early and latter rain. (James 5:7)

Likewise, the angels who gather *out* the offensive seed are also harvest angels, but their harvest is a harvest of judgment. John describes both types of harvest angels and their activities in Revelation,

> Then I looked, and behold, a white cloud, and on the cloud sat One like the Son of Man, having on His head a golden crown, and in His hand a sharp sickle. And another [*harvest*] angel came out of the temple, crying with a loud voice to Him who sat on the cloud, "Thrust in Your sickle and reap, for the time has come for You to reap, for the harvest of the earth is ripe." So He who sat on the cloud thrust in His sickle on the earth, and the earth was reaped [*the first resurrection, which is the rapture*].
>
> Then another angel [*of Judgment*] came out of the temple which is in heaven, he also having a sharp sickle. And another angel came out from the altar, who had power over fire, and he cried with a loud

cry to him who had the sharp sickle, saying, "Thrust in your sharp sickle and gather the clusters of the vine of the earth, for her grapes are fully ripe." So the angel thrust his sickle into the earth and gathered the vine of the earth, and threw it into the great winepress of the wrath of God. And the winepress was trampled outside the city, and blood came out of the winepress, up to the horses' bridles, for one thousand six hundred furlongs [*the final results of the seven bowls of wrath poured out upon the ungodly*]. (Revelation 14:14-20)

Harvest angels of judgment aren't limited to operating in the end-times. King Herod discovered this, much to his dismay. These angels execute God's judgments anytime He commands them to,

So, on a set day Herod, arrayed in royal apparel, sat on his throne and gave an oration to them. And the people kept shouting, "The voice of a god and not of a man!" Then immediately an angel of the Lord struck him, because he did not give glory to God. And he was eaten by worms and died. (Acts 12:21-23)

We should ask for the angels of harvest to go forth and bring our sons and daughters into the kingdom. Angels cannot save anyone, but they can influence them through dreams and both beneficial and adverse circumstances to cause them to turn and call upon the Lord.

Likewise, we should pray for God to execute His righteous judgments upon all governmental officials who use their positions of power and influence for selfish gain instead of serving the people who elected them. Psalm 149 says that all of God's saints have the privilege of praying God's judgments down upon corrupt leaders!

> Let the saints be joyful in glory; Let them sing aloud on their beds. Let the high praises of God be in their mouth, And a two-edged sword in their hand, To execute vengeance on the nations, And punishments on the peoples; To bind their kings with chains, And their nobles

with fetters of iron; *To execute on them the written judgment—This honor have all His saints.* Praise the Lord! (Psalm 149:5-9; italics mine)

## Resurrection Angels

Although we would seldom, if ever, need to ask for a resurrection angel, I have included them here to illustrate their importance in the Kingdom of God. As we saw previously, angels do the Father's works, so, when the last trumpet sounds and Jesus returns for the saints, these powerful angels are instrumental in raising the dead and ushering them into the eternal Kingdom! Concerning the rapture, Jesus said,

> And He will send His angels with a great sound of a trumpet, and they will gather together His elect from the four winds, from one end of heaven to the other. (Matthew 24:31)

## And Many More!

This list and commentary about the holy angels that are available to help us when we are

## Asking Specifically

in need is not exhaustive—there are many, many more! God created the heavens, which included the angels, *before* He created the earth (see Genesis 1:1). The angels were the work force who obeyed His command when He spoke to the darkness to give place to the light! They are an extension of His very being. There is no command of His that they cannot perform nor promise that they cannot fulfill. When unsure of which angels to ask for, simply ask God to send you one who will meet your need. You can be certain that He has one who can!

# Ask for the Angel

# Chapter Nine

## Evil Angels

Although Satan is traditionally seen as God's enemy, in reality, God rules over all of His creation, including all the angels and demons. Satan is *man's* enemy, not God's. Nevertheless, God promised that He would be an adversary to our adversaries and an enemy to our enemies when we walk in covenant relationship with Him. Therefore, He takes our side in our ongoing conflict with Satan and his demons and fights both for and through us when we are under attack (see Exodus 23:22).

As for Satan, he is just another arrogant, rebellious servant of God, whether he wants to be or not! He has been cast down from his original dwelling among the angels and further humiliated and defeated by Christ both in the wilderness and then through His death and subsequent resurrection. When we are under Christ's authority, as we should be, he is even subject to us. Paul prophesied that the God of peace would crush Satan under our feet shortly, and that wonderful day is fast approaching! (See Romans 16:20.)

Paul told the Corinthians to turn a certain fornicator, who was in their congregation, over to Satan for destruction of his flesh to bring him to repentance! We can be sure that Satan wasn't happy about causing someone to repent but he didn't have any choice in the matter! He is under God's authority, the same as everyone and everything else is. David said, "The Lord has established His throne in heaven, And His kingdom rules over all." That includes all the angels and demons, including Satan, himself. (see 1 Corinthians 5:1-5; Psalm 103:19)

When God sent the ten plagues upon the Egyptians to force Pharaoh to release Israel from bondage, He used "evil angels" to accomplish His task:

## Evil Angels

> He cast upon them the fierceness of his anger, wrath, and indignation, and trouble, by sending evil angels among them. (Psalm 78:49; KJV)

Then, after Moses sent the ten plagues upon Egypt and Pharaoh sent the Israelis packing, the humiliated king recanted and pursued them into the wilderness. When God opened the Red Sea before Israel, Pharaoh foolishly led his army in behind them, so, God unleashed His angels upon the Egyptians once again. This time they took their chariot wheels off to delay them until Israel reached the other side, then God closed the sea upon them, drowning them in the murky depths of the sea:

> So the children of Israel went into the midst of the sea on the dry ground, and the waters were a wall to them on their right hand and on their left. And the Egyptians pursued and went after them into the midst of the sea, all Pharaoh's horses, his chariots, and his horsemen. Now it came to pass, in the morning watch, that the Lord looked down upon

the army of the Egyptians through the pillar of fire and cloud, and He troubled the army of the Egyptians. And *He took off their chariot wheels, so that they drove them with difficulty*; and the Egyptians said, "Let us flee from the face of Israel, for the Lord fights for them against the Egyptians...." And Moses stretched out his hand over the sea; *and when the morning appeared, the sea returned to its full depth, while the Egyptians were fleeing into it.* So, the Lord overthrew the Egyptians in the midst of the sea. (Exodus 14:22-25, 27; italics mine)

God fights for His people, so, it really doesn't pay to fight against His elect! It can be quite hazardous to your health!

The fact that both angels and demons serve God equally alike is illustrated in the way God brought about Ahab's death. Micaiah gives us a behind-the-scenes look at how this was orchestrated:

Then Micaiah said, "Therefore hear the word of the Lord: *I saw the Lord sitting on*

*His throne, and all the host of heaven standing on His right hand and His left.* And the Lord said, 'Who will persuade Ahab king of Israel to go up, that he may fall at Ramoth Gilead?' So one spoke in this manner, and another spoke in that manner. Then a spirit came forward and stood before the Lord, and said, 'I will persuade him.' The Lord said to him, 'In what way?' So he said, *'I will go out and be a lying spirit in the mouth of all his prophets.'* And the Lord said, 'You shall persuade him and also prevail; *go out and do so.'* "Therefore look! *The Lord has put a lying spirit in the mouth of these prophets of yours*, and the Lord has declared disaster against you." (2 Chronicles 18:18-22; italics mine)

Throughout Scripture, that which is on God's right hand is considered good, and that which is on His left is considered bad. So, in this passage, the holy angels are standing on God's right hand, and the demons are on His left. *A lying spirit is a demon.* In fact, *it is a spirit of divination*, yet God sent this demon spirit to bring disaster upon Ahab because of His evil ways and wicked deeds.

Everyone knows about God sending Satan to be a thorn in Paul's flesh to keep him humble, but God also sent a demon spirit to afflict King Saul after he became jealous and turned against David: "But the Spirit of the Lord departed from Saul, and a distressing spirit from the Lord troubled him" (1 Samuel 16:14). Paul wrote about God's purposes for creating both angels and demons in his epistle to the Colossians:

> For this reason, we... do not cease to pray for you, and to ask that you may be filled with the knowledge of His will in all wisdom and spiritual understanding... *For by Him all things were created that are in heaven and that are on earth, visible and invisible,* whether thrones or dominions or principalities or powers. *All things were created through Him and for Him.* (Colossians 1:9, 16; italics mine)

Paul said that all things were created *by*, *through* and *for* Jesus, including all invisible beings, regardless of whether they are in heaven or on the earth. That, obviously, includes demons. In fact, Isaiah said that God "Created the spoiler to destroy" (Isaiah 54:16). Besides that, God said something else about Himself that many theologians have a hard time reconciling with their liberal theology:

> I form the light and create darkness, I make peace and create calamity; I, the Lord, do all these things.' (Isaiah 45:7)

The literal meaning of the Hebrew word *rah*, translated *calamity* in the scripture above, means evil, bad or even *wickedness!* In fact, it is translated *evil* 442 times in the KJV. So, as we said before, both holy angels and evil angels (demons) are God's servants—the important difference is not who they serve, rather it is what and why they do what they do!

There are many different theories about where demons came from. The traditional theory is they are fallen angels, who followed Satan in an early rebellion and were cast down with him. There is not much in the Bible about their source, but in this case, I tend to agree with the traditional doctrine. Both Peter and Jude said something similar about fallen angels, although neither of them called them demons:

> For if God did not spare the angels who sinned, but cast them down to hell and delivered them into chains of darkness, to be reserved for judgment. (2 Peter 2:4)

> And the angels who did not keep their proper domain, but left their own abode, He has reserved in everlasting chains under darkness for the judgment of the great day. (Jude 1:6)

Both Peter and Jude said that fallen angels are delivered into "chains of darkness for judgment", but that simply means that fallen angels (demons) cannot repent and return to the light. Once they chose to rebel, they were doomed to be cast into the lake of fire at the final judgment because there is no redemption possible for an immortal spirit. (see Matthew 8:29). Nothing can die to redeem them by taking their place, the way Jesus died in our stead! That is also one of the reasons that blaspheming the Holy Spirit is considered an unforgivable sin!

Jesus adds credibility to the belief that angels are fallen demons when He described hell and the final judgment: "Then He will also say to those on the left hand, 'Depart from Me, you cursed, into the everlasting fire prepared for the devil and his angels'." (Matthew 25:41)

Another traditionally held belief is that two thirds of the angels sided with God in the rebellion and one third fell with Satan. There is only one scripture in the entire Bible that seems to support that belief, but upon close examination it is easy to see that it does not apply to Satan's original rebellion at all. Instead, it refers to the antichrist persecuting a third of the saints in the end-times!

> And another sign appeared in heaven: behold, a great, *fiery red dragon having seven heads and ten horns*, and seven diadems on his heads. *His tail drew a third of the stars of heaven and threw them to the earth.* And the dragon stood before the woman who was ready to give birth, to

devour her Child as soon as it was born. (Revelation 12:3-4; italics mine)

The "fiery red dragon having seven heads and ten horns" is the first beast that John told us about that arises from the sea and takes dominion over the whole world! (See Revelations 13:1.) His tail, by which he pulls down a third of the stars, is the false prophet (more commonly known as the antichrist), who John also warned us about, and Isaiah tells us who the tail is! "...*The prophet who teaches lies, he is the tail*" (Isaiah 9:15). And lastly, Daniel tells us who the stars are and why the antichrist is allowed to persecute them. The only thing he doesn't tell us is how many of them will be pulled down and fall. He left that up to John:

> Those who do wickedly against the covenant he [*the antichrist, whom John also called "the false prophet"*] shall corrupt with flattery; but the people who know their God shall be strong, and carry out great exploits. And those of the people who understand shall instruct many; *yet for many days they shall fall* by sword and

flame, by captivity and plundering. Now when they fall, they shall be aided with a little help; but many shall join with them by intrigue. *And some of those of understanding shall fall, to refine them, purify them, and make them white, until the time of the end*; because it is still for the appointed time. (Daniel 11:32-35; italics mine)

Those who are wise shall shine like the brightness of the firmament, *And those who turn many to righteousness like the stars forever and ever*. (Daniel 12:3; italics mine)

So, the stars are the end-time saints. The dragon is the beast that rules the whole world, and the tail that pulls down one-third of the saints to test and try them is the false prophet who persuades the people to make an image of the beast and then commands everyone to worship it. The false prophet is the antichrist:

Then the beast was captured, and with him *the false prophet* who worked signs in his presence, by which he deceived those who received the mark of the beast *and those who worshiped his image.* These two were cast alive into the lake of fire burning with brimstone. (Revelation 19:20; italics mine)

The Bible doesn't tell us how many angels fell along with Satan in the beginning, nor should it make any difference (although we will address this subject again in the last chapter). All of them are subject to us thorough our covenant with God through our Lord Jesus Christ. Nevertheless, "the full assurance of understanding" that comes though knowing the truth strengthens our faith and faith gives us authority. Regardless of their source or how many there are, the more we can learn about them and their deceitful tactics, the better armed we are and the more successful we will be in our ongoing, unceasing warfare against them.

# Chapter Ten

## Angel Worship Forbidden

Throughout this book we have magnified the ministry of angels to teach the saints how to work closely with them to accomplish the Father's will. As we put these things into practice, it is important not to get unbalanced and exalt them above the status of servants. All of God's angels are servants. Although we should respect them and if visited by them, do whatever they instruct us to do, we are told not to worship anyone other than God, Himself!

When John made the mistake of bowing down to worship an angel who was showing him about the future, the angel quickly corrected him and told him, "See that you do not do that! Worship God!" In fact, this happened on two different occasions,

> And I fell at [*the angel's*] feet to worship him. But he said to me, *"See that you do not do that! I am your fellow servant,* and of your brethren who have the testimony of Jesus. *Worship God!* For the testimony of Jesus is the spirit of prophecy"... Now I, John... I fell down to worship before the feet of the angel who showed me these things. Then he said to me, *"See that you do not do that. For I am your fellow servant,* and of your brethren the prophets, and of those who keep the words of this book. *Worship God."* (Revelation 19:10; 22:8-9; italics mine)

Apparently, during his missionary journeys, Paul encountered ministers who were teaching the Colossians to worship angels, whose teachings Paul attributed to presumptive ignorance and pride. (They were vain, ignorant ministers who wanted to appear super-spiritual.) Paul warned the Colossians against falling into that heresy,

> Let no one cheat you of your reward,

taking delight in false humility and worship of angels, intruding into those things which he has not seen, vainly puffed up by his fleshly mind. (Colossians 2:18)

So, we see two extremes that contradict one another. Both extremes still exist in some of today's churches. One extreme is that we should command angels, and the other is that we should worship them! The Scriptures teach that we should do neither. We do not have the authority to give them commands, neither should we worship them. We are made "a little lower than the angels", but not so much lower that we should exalt and worship them. The honor of being worshiped goes to God, alone!

We should respect angels and work with them the same way we should respect and work with our fellow ministers. If we are in a fellowship of like-minded believers (as we should be), we are under the pastor and ruling elders' authority (see Hebrews 13:17; 1 Timothy 5:17). Angels also operate under their authority, in the same way a visiting minister does. In other words, the pastor can authorize a visiting minister to fully obey God without any limitations whatsoever, or ask him to teach on a certain subject, or place a certain time limit on his ministry. Likewise, with few exceptions, angels will wait for acknowledgment and permission before ministering. This is one of the main reasons we must learn to discern their presence!

If we are unaware of their presence, we may go about our traditional routine and once they see that they are not acknowledged, they will leave without giving us the benefit of their ministry. Those who are gifted to see angels often observe this scenario taking place in the churches they attend. We see this principle, of God working within the perimeters of our will, illustrated when Jesus lamented over Jerusalem because they failed to acknowledge and receive Him as their Messiah:

> O Jerusalem, Jerusalem, the one who kills the prophets and stones those who are sent to her! How often I wanted to gather your children together, as a hen

## Angel Worship Forbidden

gathers her chicks under her wings, but you were not willing! See! Your house is left to you desolate. (Matthew 23:37-38)

We can either drink from our stagnant pool of pass traditions and religious rituals or drink from the deep well of God's living waters, but we can't drink from both. The old must surrender to the new.

God ordained team ministry. Wise church leaders will ask the prophets and seers, who are the eyes and ears of the body, to freely share with them what they see and hear in a timely manner so the congregation will receive the full blessings and ministry that God intends for them to have.

God's holy angels will always reject worship. As we saw before, when John started to worship the angel that spoke to him, the angel quickly stopped him. There are biblical exceptions, such as when the Angel who appears is an epiphany—a manifestation of God, Himself. The Angel who appeared to Abraham who announced the upcoming birth of Isaac was an epiphany. This Man ate with

Abraham and discussed the overthrow of Sodom with him before leaving.

Conversely, the Angel of the Lord that was sent to announce the birth of Samson illiterates just how careful holy angels are about refusing to accept both worship and sacrifice that rightfully belongs only to the Lord:

> Then Manoah said to the Angel of the Lord, "Please let us detain You, and we will prepare a young goat for You." And the Angel of the Lord said to Manoah, "Though you detain Me, I will not eat your food. But if you offer a burnt offering, you must offer it to the Lord." (Judges 13:15-16)

On the other hand, all demons desire worship! Some demons, such as Satan, can disguise themselves as angels, so, we must be careful to discern God's holy angels from the deceivers. Satan even tried to persuade Jesus to fall down and worship him!

> Again, the devil took Him up on an exceedingly high mountain, and showed

Him all the kingdoms of the world and their glory. And he said to Him, "All these things I will give You if You will fall down and worship me." Then Jesus said to him, "Away with you, Satan! For it is written, *'You shall worship the Lord your God, and Him only you shall serve'.*" (Matthew 4:8-10; italics mine)

Paul warned the Ephesians' elders to beware of false apostles (who secretly desire to be worshiped), and when he wrote to the Corinthians, he compared false apostles to Satan, himself. (see Acts 20:29-30)

For such are false apostles, deceitful workers, transforming themselves into apostles of Christ. And no wonder! For Satan himself transforms himself into an angel of light. (2 Corinthians 11:13-14)

He also warned the saints against men and angels who preach a different gospel than the gospel that he delivered to the churches. In fact, he spoke a double curse over them!

But even if we, *or an angel from heaven,*

preach any other gospel to you than what we have preached to you, let him be accursed. As we have said before, so now I say again, if anyone preaches any other gospel to you than what you have received, let him be accursed. (Galatians 1:8-9; italics mine)

So, we are forewarned to beware of both men and angels who exalt themselves to draw away our devotion and worshipful adoration from the God and Father of our Lord Jesus Christ. Paul also warned us to reject those who preach or teach a different gospel than that which is plainly recorded in Scripture. He apparently encountered false preachers and teachers going about corrupting the gospel and deceiving the people on a frequent basis,

> But I fear, lest somehow, as the serpent deceived Eve by his craftiness, so your minds may be corrupted from the simplicity that is in Christ. For if he who comes preaches another Jesus whom we have not preached, or if you receive a different spirit which you have not

received, or a different gospel which you have not accepted—you may well put up with it! (2 Corinthians 11:3-4)

There are both "Christian" and non-Christian religions in the world today that originated by deceitful angels appearing to gullible people and introducing them to a false gospel! Beware!

## Ask for the Angel

# Chapter Eleven

## Tidbits

I had full intentions of ending this book with the preceding chapter, but after my daughter proofread the manuscript, she sent me the following text:

> Your Angel book reminded me of the time that we lost the truck keys at Chris' house, years ago. After searching high and low, I asked the Lord to send an angel to reveal where they were. Right after I prayed, I heard a clanking noise and looked where I heard it and there they were, on the floor under the loveseat. They had fallen out of it. No

## Ask for the Angel

one was even near the love-seat at that moment!

Her testimony caused me to reflect upon the number of times that I have had to ask for that same angel! I'm not sure what his name is, but he has saved the day for me more than once. I assume that he oversees God's "lost and found" department.

Although I don't identify or qualify as a "seer", I have seen angels several times and discerned their presence even more times than that. Sometimes, I knew they were present because their intervention in our affairs was the only way to explain what was happening. For instance, many years ago, before the days of self-pumping gas stations, we were moving from Louisiana to Nebraska. I was pulling a 12-foot, tandem-axle trailer with all our household belongings on it, so, my car's gas milage was rather poor. About 2:00 O'clock in the morning I started running out of gas. Since all the gas stations we passed were closed, I decided to pull over and wait until daylight. But just then,

## Tidbits

God spoke to me and said, *"Keep driving"*. Thinking there must be an open station just ahead, I obeyed. But soon the gas needle started getting very close to empty, so, being afraid of having to leave my family while I hitchhiked to get gas, I started to stop once again. This time His voice was quite firm—He said, *"I said, keep driving!"*

I nervously obeyed. *We drove for about two and one-half hours on an empty gas tank* before finally coming to an all-night truck-stop! I put 21.7 gallons of gasoline into a car that only held 21 gallons! Even the gas lines must have been empty! God spoke. I obeyed. His angels performed the miracle. There is no other explanation possible!

Another time, in total ignorance, I was using a broom to scrub grease from a concrete floor using several gallons of gasoline as a cleaning fluid. I was in a large, enclosed basement. As I learned later, gasoline fumes are heavier than air—and except for the angels, my lack of knowledge would have led to a catastrophic ending—because a gas boiler in the basement suddenly lit and set the gasoline fumes on fire. As the explosion swept through the basement, in utter amazement, I watched the flames divide and completely surround me, even setting the broom that I held in my hands on fire. Yet, I felt no heat and not a hair on my body was singed. The 10-foot ceiling above my head was set ablaze but the pan of gasoline at my feet never ignited. I walked out of the basement completely unscathed. Only angels can perform such amazing feats! Even the fireman who responded to extinguish the blaze were bewildered to explain what happened.

In the second chapter I wrote about God telling me that Joshua's vanguard angel was named Toronto. He also gave me another angel's name. This time, in a dream. I have a brother named Alvin, who, like myself, has devoted his life to ministry and the study of God's word. I live in Louisiana, and he lives in Arkansas. He was coming to see me one weekend and the morning he was scheduled to arrive, I dreamed that his angel accompanied him as he drove and gave him a revelation from the word. His angel's name was Pac-r-ram. God even spelled his name for me. So, when my brother arrived, I asked him, "What revelation did your angel give you on your way down?" He was startled. He asked, "How did you know that I had a revelation?" I told him that I saw Pac-r-ram talking to him in a dream. On a side note, his angel not only had a unique name, his appearance was unique too. His head and body appeared to be made of living Plexiglass and were geometric in shape.

I have a few more interesting angelic encounters to share, but I will save them for another book. Meanwhile, the following is something interesting to think about. Usually when I teach or write about something, I am very careful to avoid interjecting any extra-biblical content into the subject, but I am about to make an exception to my own rule. I have a theory about guardian angels that I would like to share with you. Since it is only a theory, and cannot be biblically proven, simply judge for yourself whether you think it is right or not. It is about what happens when we are young and we commit our first willful sin, and, like Adam, become separated from God.

Jesus said, "Likewise, I say to you, there is joy in the presence of the angels of God over one sinner who repents" (Luke 15:10). My theory goes like this—when we are young and first fall into temptation and sin, we are no longer found innocent and blameless before God. I believe that at that point in time we are separated from our guardian angel and lose his protection and assistance. The moment we are saved, we are reunited with him. As a result, there is an occasion for great rejoicing in heaven!

To me, this explains why we can drift so far from God and even be unaware of our danger. Our willful disobedience has separated us from the angel charged with overseeing our well-being. Of course, it is only a theory, so, who knows? Some beautiful day soon, we will all know even as we are now known.

While we are still in a speculation mode, there is another tidbit that I will present to you for your consideration. We have already shown that the traditional doctrine of God having two thirds of the angels on His side, leaving Satan with the rebellious leftovers, is based upon a misinterpretation and misapplication of an end-time scripture found in John's Revelation. But there *is* a scripture that may give us a hint as to the actual distribution of angels—Jesus asked His disciples, "Are there not twelve hours in the day?" (John 11:9).

If there are twelve hours in the day, it doesn't take a mathematician to calculate the number of hours in the night. Actually, there are only two days in each year when the twenty-four-hour day is equally divided in half (known as the equinox), so there is a hidden message in Jesus' rhetorical question—He is actually pointing out that light and darkness are exact opposites—the difference being that light is far superior to darkness. Light *always* dominates and displaces darkness! So, the implication is that angelic forces are equally divided in number, but not equal in power!

This explains another of my observations into the angelic realm—for every positive, there is a negative. In other words, since demons are fallen angels, almost every specific type of angel appears to have a corresponding, opposing type of demon. For example, Raphael is a type of healing angel who can heal any sickness or disease. Likewise, there are demonic spirits who can afflict people with any known (or unknown) sickness or disease, such as the woman with a spirit of infirmity (*idiopathic scoliosis?*), whom Jesus loosed from bondage:

> And behold, there was a woman who had a spirit of infirmity eighteen years, and was bent over and could in no way raise herself up. But when Jesus saw her, He called her to Him and said to her, "Woman, you are loosed from your infirmity." And He laid His hands on

her, and immediately she was made straight, and glorified God. [*Then, in response to the synagogue ruler's criticism of Him healing the woman on the Sabbath, He asked,*] "So ought not this woman, being a daughter of Abraham, whom Satan has bound—think of it—for eighteen years, be loosed from this bond on the Sabbath?" (Luke 13:11-13, 16)

This is confirmed by Luke's brief, but concise description of Jesus' ministry:

How God anointed Jesus of Nazareth with the Holy Spirit and with power, who went about doing good and *healing all who were oppressed by the devil*, for God was with Him. (Acts 10:38; italics mine)

So, if holy angels can calm the winds and still the raging sea, as we discussed in chapter 8, then fallen angels can send the storm that threatened to sink the boat in the first place! Fallen angels of prosperity oppose people and afflict them with everything from bankruptcy in businesses to divorce in marriage. The spirit of bondage was originally created as an enforcer of liberty. Demons of strife and contention are fallen angels who were originally created to assure peace and harmony among men. Demons of grief and depression were created to fill the earth with joy and rejoicing! This *reversal of what they were created to do* is possible because *any spirit that can enhance or inflame an emotion or desire can suppress, dull or deaden that same emotion or desire.*

Understanding and applying this *principle of reversal* helps to reveal the unseen, invisible things of the spirit realm. For example, I have discerned the spirit of doubt hindering people from being able to believe and receive their healing numerous times. Since there is *a demon of doubt*, there must also be *an angel of faith* that we can ask for. As God said, "It doesn't hurt to ask for the angel", and we could all use more faith! Although Paul didn't call the "spirit of faith" an angel, he did mention this spirit in one of his epistles (see: 2 Corinthians 4:13). So, whether this spirit is an angel or are a unique anointing of the Holy Spirit, it behooves us to ask for it.

There is another aspect of *reversal* that we need to consider. The Lord once told me, "I can't give you the power to raise the dead without giving you the power to kill the living". Why? Because the same angel who has the power to restore life also has the power to take life. These angels are the ones who spared the Israelites on the night of Passover and in the process killed the firstborn of every Egyptian family. They will also assist Christ in gathering in the saints when the final trumpet blows and the dead are raised during the rapture, which we discussed in chapter 8.

The prince of darkness, whom Paul said works in the sons of disobedience, was originally created as an angel of light. This explains why Paul said that he is still able to appear as such: "And no wonder! For Satan himself transforms himself into an angel of light". (2 Corinthians 11:14—also see Isaiah

14:12-14; Ephesians 2:2-3)

As seen in the example given above, fallen angels still have the ability to continue doing what they were originally created to do, but with a sinister, wicked twist. One can see this by examining the way demons work who were originally created as angels of wisdom. In addition to causing some people to be confused in their thoughts and stumbling in their speech, and others to be outright fools, these clever demons can enable men to be evasive, subtle and deceptively wise. They are active in everything from political campaigns to financial scams. They also work in cooperation with demons of covetousness in conmen to cheat others through pyramid and Ponzi schemes. James said,

> Who is wise and understanding among you? Let him show by good conduct that his works are done in the meekness of wisdom. But if you have bitter envy and *self-seeking in your hearts,* do not boast and lie against the truth. *This wisdom does*

*not descend from above, but is earthly, sensual, demonic.* For where envy and *self-seeking exist, confusion and every evil thing are there.* But the wisdom that is from above is first pure, then peaceable, gentle, willing to yield, full of mercy and good fruits, without partiality and without hypocrisy. (James 3:13-17; italics mine; also see 2 Peter 2:1-3)

Beware of this demon! Paul spoke of deceived men who considered themselves wise, but in reality, they were fools (see Romans 1:22). Today's political arena is inundated with corrupt, self-seeking officials who are deceived and motivated by these demons.

Woe to those who call evil good, and good evil; Who put darkness for light, and light for darkness; Who put bitter for sweet, and sweet for bitter! *Woe to those who are wise in their own eyes, And prudent in their own sight!* (Isaiah 5:20-21; italics mine)

## Ask for the Angel

As we saw in the example of the angel with power to both raise the dead and kill the living, this principle of reversal isn't limited to demons. God's holy angels also have the ability to operate on both ends of the spectrum. This is seen in the operation of a unique angel that John called *"the angel of the waters"*. After the rapture, during the time when God pours out His wrath upon the ungodly, this angel will turn the rivers and springs of fresh water into blood to punish those who have persecuted the righteous.

> And I heard *the angel of the waters* saying: "You are righteous, O Lord, The One who is and who was and who is to be, Because You have judged these things. For they have shed the blood of saints and prophets, And You have given them blood to drink. For it is their just due." (Revelation 16:5-6; italics mine)

Undoubtedly, this "angel of the waters", that can turn rivers into blood, is the same angel who worked with Elisha to purify the polluted waters of Jericho:

> Then the men of the city said to Elisha, "Please notice, the situation of this city is pleasant, as my lord sees; but the water is bad, and the ground barren." And he said, "Bring me a new bowl, and put salt in it." So they brought it to him. Then he went out to the source of the water, and cast in the salt there, and said, "Thus says the Lord: 'I have healed this water; from it there shall be no more death or barrenness.' " So the water remains healed to this day, according to the word of Elisha which he spoke. (2 Kings 2:19-22)

The primary symbolic meaning of salt is *grace*. In response to Elisha's prophetic act and spoken word, the angel graciously "healed" Jericho's polluted waters and barren landscape.

As we saw before, the warrior angels under Toronto were able to put the fear and dread of meeting the Israelites upon the Canaanites and at the same time give Joshua great boldness for the encounter! They were able to inflame the emotion of fear in the Canaanites and suppress fear in Joshua's men. This observation also explains why their Captain's name is Toronto (meaning: *"the meeting place"*), instead of something like Phobos (*fear*) or Deimos (*dread*), which it would be if his ministry was limited to imposing fear and dread upon his subjects. (Both the name Toronto and its definition are derived from the Mohawk word *"tkaronto — where there are trees standing in the water"*.)

In summary, using today's unique vernacular, there are 32 specific angel types who chose the dark side, who now identify as demons. (Please don't ask me to explain!)

So, in the final analysis, it isn't what angels and demons do, or are capable of doing, that identifies them, it is the fruits of their ministry. To properly identify them we should ask ourselves questions such as, *"Is what they are doing edifying? Is it helpful or harmful?"* And most important of all, *"Who are they glorifying?"*

## Tidbits

Jesus said,

> He who speaks from himself seeks his own glory; but He who seeks the glory of the One who sent Him is true, and no unrighteousness is in Him. (John 7:18)

Jesus warned us to beware of wolves in sheep's clothing. He said, "You will know them by their fruits" (Matthew 7:16). The identity of both men and demons is revealed by their works and both the demons and those who are deceived and motivated by them will be rewarded accordingly.

And last, but not least, in the same way that angels work together in teams to fulfill the Father's will, demons often do the same (or rather, in the case of demons, it is more appropriate to say that *they work together in packs!*) For instance, demons of strife and contention often work in conjunction with demons who cause alcohol or drug addictions. Their purpose is to inflame friends and family with anger and hatred toward one another, causing divorce and separation among family members. They are adapt at provoking everything from bar fights to church splits! As in nature, the wolves know that those who are separated from the herd are easy prey compared to those who gain support from one another.

Jesus explained how demons who are cast out summon others to help them regain their former place (or "house"):

> When an unclean spirit goes out of a man, he goes through dry places, seeking rest; and finding none, he says, "I will return to my house from which I came." And when he comes, he finds it swept and put in order. Then he goes and takes with him seven other spirits more wicked than himself, and they enter and dwell there; and the last state of that man is worse than the first. (Luke 11:24-26)

After he is cast out, he howls for the whole

wolf-pack to convene! So, knowing this, when you ask God for angelic assistance, don't limit yourself to just one or two—ask for the whole team! (This may help explain why Jesus spoke of His Father supplying Him with twelve legions of angels instead of just a handful of warriors.)

So, with that mouth-full to chew on, I leave you with Paul's beautiful admonition to his beloved son Timothy, which has nothing, and everything, to do with angels!

> But you, O man of God, flee these [vain, temporal, materialistic] things and pursue righteousness, godliness, faith, love, patience, gentleness. Fight the good fight of faith, lay hold on eternal life, to which you were also called and have confessed the good confession in the presence of many witnesses.
>
> I urge you in the sight of God who gives life to all things, and before Christ Jesus who witnessed the good confession

before Pontius Pilate, that you keep this commandment without spot, blameless until our Lord Jesus Christ's appearing, which He will manifest in His own time, He who is the blessed and only Potentate, the King of kings and Lord of lords, who alone has immortality, dwelling in unapproachable light, whom no man has seen or can see, to whom be honor and everlasting power. Amen. (1 Timothy 6:11-16)

*Other Titles by* Ira Milligan

# Understanding the Dreams You Dream

*Biblical Keys for Hearing God's Voice in the Night*

God frequently talks through dreams. The Bible reveals that in the past, dreams were the most common way God talked to His people. Unlike the early Christians, today's believers often treat dreams like junk mail. In doing so, they often throw away the very answers they ask for when they pray for counsel and guidance. *Understanding the Dreams You Dream* is written from a Christian perspective to help Christians understand the symbolic language of dreams. Deliberately written without technical jargon, this book can be easily understood and used by everyone. It is the only complete, one volume Christian reference book for interpreting dreams on the market today.

# The Ultimate Guide to Understanding the Dreams You Dream

*Biblical Keys for Hearing God's Voice in the Night*

*The Ultimate Guide* provides insight into your dreams–and your life! Two books in one, it includes a comprehensive dictionary of dream symbols to guide you through the complex world of dreams.

Best-selling author and minister Ira Milligan has decades of personal experience interpreting dreams of his own and those of others. He uses biblical examples to illustrate the way God uses dreams to communicate to His people. This book gives you *Biblical Keys for Hearing God's Voice in the Night* through:

- Specific, detailed directions about hearing God's voice.
- A comprehensive A-Z dictionary of symbol definitions.
- Discerning the difference between dreams God gives and those from other sources. Both normal and abnormal dream situations are presented, enabling you to interpret your own dreams.

# The Church Triumphant

## *Strategies for War*

Malachi prophesied that the day was coming when, *"The Sun of Righteousness shall arise With healing in His wings... You shall trample the wicked, For they shall be ashes under the soles of your feet On the day that I do this, Says the Lord of hosts"* (Malachi 4:2-3). Malachi's, *"You shall trample the wicked, For they shall be ashes under the soles of your feet"* exactly parallels Paul's promise, *"And the God of peace will crush Satan under your feet shortly"* (Romans 16:20). The church has been waiting and longing for Paul's *shortly* to come to pass now for centuries and that wonderful day has finally arrived, along with its miraculous healings, abundant provision and resounding victory—it is an exciting day to be alive! *The Church Triumphant* offers numerous innovative strategies for obtaining victory in this war

# Practical Christianity

## *Rediscovering the*

## *New Testament Church*

This book is a field manual for effective spiritual warfare. God's mighty army is disorganized and uncertain of how to fight against the subtle and deceptive hit-and-run tactics the enemy is using. This book's twofold purpose is to provide a biblical training manual to raise up an effective fighting force for war along with detailed instructions for making a new wineskin to serve the new wine that God has for this generation. Our old wineskin cannot contain or sustain the billion soul, end-time harvest that God has planned. To fight and win a billion souls to Christ and then lose them from the lack of a trained work force to nurture and disciple them would be a catastrophic loss! The time to prepare is now.

# UNDERSTANDING
## the Book of
# REVELATION

*Blessed is He Who Reads and Those Who Hear the Words of This Prophesy*

There is no other book in the Bible that has captured the interest and imagination of God's saints like John's Revelation. Also, there is no other book that promises a special blessing upon those who read and keep its word, but therein lies the rub—very few understand its structure and symbolism, so many are unable to heed its instructions! This book will guide the reader through Revelations' intriguing, interwoven, end-time mysteries and show the victorious, conquering Christ that it reveals.

# UNDERSTANDING
## the Book of
# REVELATION
## Study Guide

This *Study Guide* is a companion to *UNDERSTANDING the Book of REVELATION*. It is written to assist the reader in organizing and understanding the many different issues that one is faced with when studying John's Revelation. It will enable the reader to see, at a glance, the historical settings for the seven seals and their relationship to the seven church ages as they have unfolded in history. Also, it will help the reader discern where we are in Revelation's historical timeline, and what we can expect to experience in the near future as John's prophecies continue to unfold upon the world scene.

# The Master's Voice

*A Practical Guide to Personal Ministry*

Someone once said, "Experience is the best teacher," and as long as it's someone else's experience, it is! Some things, like ministering the gifts of the Spirit, are *only* learned from personal experience, but it helps to have a few hints along the way. This book is written to share the lessons learned from over thirty years of personal ministry. Both instructional and inspirational, Ira has intermingled a delightful array of Scriptural illustrations and personal, real-life experiences to enlighten and inform the reader. Whether you are a seasoned veteran or a complete novice when it comes to operating spiritual gifts, this book is for you.


# Rightly Dividing the Word

*Illustrating A Perfect Heart*

One of God's favorite tactics to hide truth is to place it in plain sight but disguise it as something other than what it is. Almost all spiritual truth is first clothed with a natural disguise. When we remove the natural covering, we find the naked truth! Like wheat, the natural husk must be removed from the grain before it is usable. An example of this is Moses' Law. The Law is spiritual, but it is clothed with various commandments and ordinances that hide its precious truths. These spiritual treasures are *"life unto those that find them, and health to all their flesh"* (Proverbs 4:23). *Rightly Dividing the Word* carefully guides the serious Bible student step by step through the Scriptures to safely obtain these treasures.

# Hidden Mysteries of the Bible, Vol. I

*A Foundational Bible Study Course (52 Lessons)*

The Bible is filled with wonderful paradoxes, seeming contradictions, perplexing parables and intriguing mysteries. One reason for its sometimes difficult but always fascinating makeup is it is composed of two interwoven, parallel journeys that are often confused with one another. One is natural, the other is spiritual. Both contain precious promises, but one is accomplished by merit, the other by grace. This fifty-two lesson *Bible Study Course* guides the student step by step, all the way from the tragic fall of Adam to man's glorious restoration in Christ.

# Hidden Mysteries of the Bible, Vol. II

*A Foundational Bible Study Course (52 Lessons)*

The ability to see into spiritual darkness and positively discern the presence and identity of demons is invaluable. Demons love darkness because they *are* darkness. They are completely repelled by light, and God is light! Effective warfare starts with under-standing one's enemy, and spiritual warfare is no exception. Our war with Satan goes beyond our personal battles with him. John said he deceives whole nations. This in-depth Bible course reveals both Satan's tactics and his weaknesses to give God's people a much-needed advantage in their warfare with him.

# Understanding Bible Mysteries

*The Truth Shall Make You Free*

A wise Christian historian once observed, every major heresy began as a minor deviation from the truth. Heresy is an insidious parasite, thriving by feeding upon the truth. Like counterfeit money, it cannot exist alone. It has to have the substance of truth to survive. Although the consequence of doctrinal error may seem relatively minor in the beginning, the actual harm and damage becomes apparent as it is magnified by time and sustained by tradition.

In Ephesians 4:14, Paul admonished the Saints to "Be no more children, tossed to and fro, and carried about with every wind of doctrine", but today's Church has been tossed to and fro like a derelict ship on stormy seas. *Understanding Bible Mysteries* calms the winds and straightens the sails to restore balance and stability to the storm-tossed ship.

# The Hidden Power of Covenant

*Releasing the Fullness of the Blessing of the Gospel of Jesus Christ*

Paul wrote to the church in Rome and boldly declared, "And I am sure that, when I come unto you, I shall come in the fulness of the blessing of the gospel of Christ" (Rom. 15:29). How could he be so sure? In fact, the New King James Version of the Bible translates Paul as saying, "I *know* that when I come to you, I shall come in the fullness of the blessing..." How could he be so confident? What did he know that made him so bold? And, besides that, just what *is* the *fulness of the blessing* of the gospel, anyway? The answers are hidden deep in the mystery of covenant. This book probes and explores this mystery to reveal the surprising answers to these important questions.

# The Four Winds

*Illustrating The Four Winds of Heaven*

*The Four Winds* defines and illustrates the four winds of Heaven as they oppose the four winds of the earth (Dan. 7:2; Rev. 7:1). As the story of this ancient conflict unfolds, the role of the prophetic and apostolic ministries in the end-time church is both clarified and explained. The restoration of the prophetic and apostolic ministries is part of God's end-time promise to *restore "all things prophesied by the prophets from the beginning of time"* (Acts 3:21). *The Four Winds* exposes and defines several changes necessary before this promise can be realized.

# The Scorpion Within

## *Illustrating The Wheel of Nature*

*"Behold, I give unto you power to tread on serpents and scorpions, and over all the power of the enemy"* (Luke 10:19). Most Christians know that *serpents* symbolize demons, but very few know the truth and power that lies hidden in the *scorpion's* symbolism. *The Scorpion Within* unveils this mystery and reveals its practical application for every believer. A must for anyone interested in counseling and deliverance (this book is accompanied by a separate counselor's aid--*The Wheel of Nature*).

# Life Transformation

## *Finding Peace and Happiness in*

## *Today's Fast-Paced, Stressful World*

*Life Transformation* reveals the causes of dysfunctional, stressful thinking and living that are so common to today's society. The first four chapters of the Bible gives us understanding of both the causes and cures of most of societies' maladies and ills that afflict us all. This book reveals the Scriptures' clear, simple instructions to obtain lasting peace and happiness in our lives.

# The Twelve Universal Laws
## that Govern the Universe

The twelve universal, spiritual laws that govern our lives in everything we say and do are like gravity, they are impartial, infallible and immutable. They are unwavering and relentless in their pursuit of equality and justice. Understanding them gives us an edge in our constant warfare against our common enemy—Satan and his demonic hoards. Being ignorant of them handicaps us and presents many difficulties and hindrances in our attempts to please and serve the Lord Jesus.

Many of these books may be ordered directly from my website. Some that are self-published are not listed in my web-page book store.

These may be ordered by

emailing me at:

iralmilligan@gmail.com

or by contacting

me at the

address below.

*Servant Ministries Inc.*

PO Box 1120

Tioga LA, 71477

www.servant-ministries.org

www.ingramcontent.com/pod-product-compliance
Lightning Source LLC
LaVergne TN
LVHW010326070526
838199LV00065B/5675